Puffin Books

The Luck of Troy

When Nicostratus was only two he and his mother, the beautiful Helen of Sparta, were carried off from Greece by Prince Paris of Troy. Ten years later, when this story begins, the long, weary, bitter siege of Troy is drawing to a close, and Nico, brought up in Troy but nourished on stories of Greece, hardly knows which side he belongs to.

But he discovers that the Greek hero Achilles has secretly entered Troy to ask for the hand of Polyxena the Trojan Princess, and that Paris is planning to betray him. He cannot save Achilles, but from then onwards he swears he will help the Greek army to capture Troy.

In the Trojan temple is a little, black stone statue of Pallas Athena, and the legend runs that the city which held it could never be conquered: this is the Luck of Troy, and Nico, too young to fight in this war of heroes, can help Odysseus by smuggling the image out of Troy . . .

Roger Lancelyn Green knows exactly how to blend excitement with fascinating historical fact and legend. This is a thrilling story for readers of ten to twelve.

Cover design by Philip Gough

ROGER LANCELYN GREEN

The Luck of Troy

Illustrated by
Margery Gill

Puffin Books
in association with
The Bodley Head

Puffin Books, Penguin Books Ltd, Harmondsworth, Middlesex, England
Penguin Books, 625 Madison Avenue, New York, New York 10022, U.S.A.
Penguin Books Australia Ltd, Ringwood, Victoria, Australia
Penguin Books Canada Ltd, 2801 John Street, Markham, Ontario, Canada L3R 1B4
Penguin Books (N.Z.) Ltd, 182–190 Wairau Road, Auckland 10, New Zealand

First published by The Bodley Head, 1961
Published in Puffin Books 1967
Reprinted 1971, 1973, 1975, 1977, 1983

Copyright © Roger Lancelyn Green, 1961
Illustrations copyright © The Bodley Head, 1961

Made and printed in Great Britain by
Richard Clay (The Chaucer Press) Ltd,
Bungay, Suffolk
Set in Monotype Centaur

TO SCIRARD

CONTENTS

THE CHARACTERS

MENELAUS married HELEN and became King of Sparta. They had one daughter, HERMIONE, and a son, NICOSTRATUS. Helen's sister, CLYTEMNESTRA, married AGAMEMNON, King of Mycenae, brother of Menelaus, and their children were IPHIGENEIA, ELECTRA and ORESTES. Helen's cousin PENELOPE married ODYSSEUS, King of Ithaca.

PRIAM, King of Troy, married HECUBA (sister of THEANO the priestess of Athena and guardian of the Palladion — the *Luck of Troy*), and their children included HECTOR, PARIS, DEIPHOBUS and HELENUS, and two daughters POLYXENA and CASSANDRA. Among Priam's most trusted councillors were ANTENOR, husband of Theano, and his cousin ANCHISES, father of AENEAS.

Priam's sister HESIONE was the second wife of TELAMON, the Greek, whose son AJAX was the strongest of the Greek heroes who attacked Troy. Besides AGAMEMNON, who was in command of the whole expedition, the chief Greek kings and warriors were ACHILLES, son of Peleus — and later his son NEOPTOLEMUS; PATROCLUS, cousin and best friend of Achilles; old NESTOR, King of Pylos; ODYSSEUS, wisest of the Greeks; DIOMEDES; ECHION; IDOMENEUS, son of Minos, King of Crete; and PALAMEDES, Prince of Nauplia, the sea-port of Mycenae.

No character in the story is invented. Even KILISSA, the nurse of Agamemnon's children, appears in old age in *The Choephoroe* of Aeschylus. The letter written by PALAMEDES is in Mycenaean Greek, in the script known as 'Linear B' in which many tablets survive that were written at the actual date of the Trojan War.

PROLOGUE AT MYCENAE

The day had been long, hot and tiring. Even Iphigeneia, who was twelve, was almost exhausted, and her sister Electra, a good four years younger, looked white and drawn, though she refused to admit she had had enough.

As for their little cousin Hermione, who was barely six, she had fainted during the slow procession from the Lion Gate, along the sun-baked hillside towards the great bee-hive tomb, and had been carried back to the Palace in the citadel of Mycenae and had missed all the more interesting parts of the funeral of her grandfather, the old King Atreus.

But she was wide awake now after her long sleep during the heat of the day, and eager to hear about all that had happened before the tomb was walled up and King Atreus left alone to make his long journey to the Realm of Hades.

'Come down into the New Court,' said Iphigeneia, 'it's beautifully cool there, and we won't be disturbed for ages. I'll ask Kilissa to bring us some grapes and honey-cakes, and we can get lovely cold water from the cistern.'

Together the three girls went out of the palace by a side entrance and along the path over the brow of the hill. As they came into the sunlight a tall guard in a bronze helmet and quilted armour stood smartly to attention and saluted. They did not speak to him, and did not even seem to notice as he hitched his big figure-of-eight shield over his shoulder, took up his spear and followed them at a respectful distance.

Iphigeneia led the way down a flight of steps between buildings and then by an even steeper stair into an open courtyard with high walls of huge stones all round it. At one end a pointed doorway led down the long steps to the underground water-cistern, and at the other a narrow gap in the thick outer wall — the new sally-port which young King Agamemnon had just built — was blocked by a huge door studded with bronze.

The three girls settled themselves comfortably in a little alcove which formed the top of the watch-tower at the north-east corner of the New Court. Behind them the wall curved round over the edge of the rocks above the deep gorge through which splashed the mountain torrent of the little river Chonia, and there was a roof of baked reddish-yellow tiles to shield them from the sun. But there was no barrier on the inside, and sitting back in the shadow they could look out to the south-west over the wall beyond the new courtyard and away down the valley to the wide plain of Argos, where the leaves of the olive trees flashed pale silver in the sunlight, and to the far-away mountains of Arcadia beyond.

Iphigeneia settled herself comfortably in a corner and put her hands behind her head.

'Oh, Artemis, I am tired!' she exclaimed. 'But I wouldn't have missed it. Even though it was a bit frightening to see grandfather's body in its gold mask laid down on the stone in that little dark room, with his sword and dagger beside him, and all the jars and caskets. And when we drank the Cup of Farewell, and father let it fall to the floor and break into pieces, I almost wanted to scream.'

'Then we came out into the big dim Tholos,' said Electra in her slow deep voice. 'It's such a wonderful room: quite round and going up to a point at the top, ever so far above – I couldn't really see the point. It *is* just like a bee-hive ... And when we were all quiet we could hear a swarm of bees buzzing up in the dome: that made me feel all shivery and solemn.'

'It was odd, too, coming out into the sunshine,' said Iphigeneia thoughtfully. 'Such a sudden change. And Orestes began crying: Kilissa was carrying him, but mother took him quickly and managed to get him to sleep again.'

'It seems rather strange to take a baby to the funeral,' remarked Hermione in her gentle way. 'Even children don't go, at home in Sparta.'

'Ah, but Orestes is the only grandson, you see,' explained Electra importantly. 'He'll be the next king of Mycenae and Overlord of Achaia after father: so of course he had to be there. It's strange to think that when he's a very old man, and dies, he'll be buried there too.'

'And his grandson,' said Hermione, her eyes big and solemn.

'Oh no,' said Electra. 'His grandson will probably think there are enough bones in the tomb by then, and he'll wall up the doorway and bury it all under earth, with only a ring of stones over the very top to mark the place – just like the stones down in the Front Court by the Lion Gate where the ancient kings were buried, oh, long before even Perseus. Only they didn't have a big round Tholos like a huge bee-hive, but just the little room cut in the rock and roofed over. Do you have nice big tombs in Sparta?'

Hermione sighed. 'Father did begin to build one,' she

said, 'but I don't expect he'll go on with it now – unless he gets mother and Nicostratos back.'

'Oh, do tell us what really happened!' exclaimed Electra eagerly. 'Of course we've heard bits of it, but we don't really know anything for certain. I asked mother, but she was so cross that I can't ask her again. Kilissa has a wonderful story about the Trojan prince Paris taking on the shape of Uncle Menelaus by magic and telling Aunt Helen that she must come with him on a voyage to Crete – I forget why. But whatever did happen, it's awfully exciting, and I heard father say there would probably be a big war against Troy. There hasn't been a war for such a long time, except for one very small rebellion down over there at Argos.'

'I don't think it's a bit exciting,' said Hermione, 'and it's horrid of you to talk like that, Electra. Just think if it was your mother, Queen Clytemnestra, who had been stolen away, and your little brother who had been taken too.'

'I wouldn't mind a bit,' declared Electra defiantly. 'Mother's often unkind to me. She spoils Orestes like anything, and he's such a little cry baby!'

'Electra, really!' exclaimed Iphigeneia, looking quite shocked. 'It's wicked to say that about mother. And it's certainly unkind to poor little Hermione to talk about what's happened to Aunt Helen just as if it were one of the tales which the minstrel chants in the megaron after dinner.'

'Well, I expect the minstrels will be singing about the beautiful Queen Helen who was carried off to Troy by Prince Paris,' cried Electra, who hated to be found fault with by anyone. 'But I didn't mean to hurt your feelings, Hermione. I just wanted to know what really happened, that's all. And if there is going to be a great war against Troy, with kings and heroes from all over Greece and the islands doing mighty deeds, of course we want to know all about how it started. And I think it's rather fun to be really *in* it: that's why I wish it had been mother and not Aunt Helen who'd been carried off. But of course Aunt Helen's the most beautiful woman in the world. Why, the minstrels are already singing about her, and the way all the suitors came to Sparta to seek her hand in marriage, and how Theseus the famous old King of Athens carried her away and she had to be rescued by Menelaus the brave young prince of Mycenae, and Odysseus of Ithaca, and the rest of them.'

'It was after she was rescued that all the kings and princes who were her suitors swore the oath to punish anyone who stole her again, wasn't it?' said Iphigeneia, who was really just as interested as Electra in the adventures of their aunt, Helen of Sparta.

Hermione herself could not help feeling proud that the most beautiful woman in all Greece was her mother, or that a great war might be started for her sake. So it was with pride mixed with sadness that she replied to her cousins' questions.

'It's not mother's fault. Zeus made her so beautiful and so gentle and kind that everybody loves her. And I suppose it is rather exciting to be in an adventure like this – only it doesn't make me miss her any less, or baby Nico either.' Hermione paused, and there were tears in her eyes. But a moment later she went on.

'It was very odd and strange, certainly. Paris came in one of those Trojan ships with a big red sail. We drove down to Gytheion with six chariots to welcome him: father let me come in his own chariot, so we went first and there was hardly any dust. But it was very uncomfortable driving for twenty miles without stopping. However, it was worth it when we got there, for the Trojan ship was the biggest one I've ever seen. And it was so odd to see all the sailors with their funny Phrygian caps and tunics, and all of them so brown. But Prince Paris was much more like a Greek, and he's very handsome – almost too handsome, father said, meaning that he was almost pretty, with big eyes and small hands: he called him a beautiful barbarian! Well, Paris came back to Sparta with his friend Aeneas and several of the young Trojan nobles who had come with him. And there was feasting, and even some chariot racing and games. I didn't see the Trojans very much, of course, after that day at Gytheion: but I heard a lot about them.'

Hermione paused, and Iphigeneia asked, 'Why had they come to Greece at all? A prince of Troy would hardly be trading like a merchant, surely?'

'Well, father did say that all Trojans were merchants first, and men afterwards,' said Hermione. 'But he may just have been joking; and I don't think he liked Paris right from the start. Paris never talked about trading or anything like that, and he was really rather nice whenever I saw him. And he sang very well, such strange Eastern songs, like the slave-girls from Lydia sing.'

'But didn't your mother like him?' asked Electra.

Hermione shivered suddenly. 'I don't think she really liked him,' she answered, 'but she was – what's it called – fascinated by him: yes, like a mouse sitting up and looking at a cat, or a bird hopping jerkily towards a snake . . . Yes, she was frightened of him.'

Hermione stopped, and Electra exclaimed eagerly, 'Go on! How did he persuade her to go away with him?'

'She didn't!' cried Hermione. 'Oh how horrid you are! He took her away: it was a drug. Yes, your Kilissa was right when she said he used magic . . . I've heard that in Asia they worship Hecate the Queen Witch – well, they do in Colchis, anyhow. Paris must have got the drug from one of the witches who serve her.'

'What happened?' asked Iphigeneia.

'Father had to go away suddenly to Crete,' said Hermione. 'It was something to do with the death of old King Catreus. There's always trouble in Crete, father says. Well, it was the very night after he'd gone that – that Paris stole mother and Nico away.'

'Why ever didn't King Menelaus insist on Paris setting sail the same time as he did?' asked Electra.

'Yes,' agreed Iphigeneia. 'They'd have started the same way, wouldn't they? Round as far as Cape Malea, anyhow.'

'Paris wasn't going by sea,' explained Hermione. 'Didn't I tell you? Oh no. Well, you see he said that his father, King Priam of Troy, had sent him to Greece to find out how his aunt was. That's old Hesione, the second wife of King Telamon of Salamis. Old King Telamon won her as a prize, or something, when he helped Heracles to conquer Troy, oh ages ago. Well, Paris was going to stay one more night, and then set out very early next morning, and get at least as far as Tegea that night, if not to Argos or here, on his way to Athens. But he didn't. Perhaps it was all a lie.'

Hermione stopped again, and Iphigeneia remarked, 'It was quite true about Hesione, I've heard father talk about her. And of course she comes into some of the lays about Heracles which the minstrels sing: Heracles is supposed to have saved her from a sea-monster, just as Perseus saved Andromeda.'

'You still haven't told us what really happened,' interrupted Electra impatiently. 'Old tales about Heracles are all very well, but this is much more real. Heracles died so long ago I can hardly believe in him — but I've actually seen Aunt Helen!'

'Of course you have!' laughed Iphigeneia. 'You really are funny, Electra. You'll be saying next that you really believe in father, Agamemnon, the King of Mycenae and Lord of the Achaians — but you don't believe in Paris, prince of Troy, because you've never seen him!'

'No, but Hermione has,' snapped Electra. 'Be quiet, I want to hear how he carried off Aunt Helen!'

'It was like a horrible dream,' Hermione shivered. 'Mother kissed me good night as usual, and as I fell asleep I could hear her singing a lullaby to Nico: although he's nearly two, she still sings it to him just as she did when he was a tiny baby. When I woke up again it was quite dark, but the full moon was shining brightly. Mother was dressed, and as I watched her moving about the room I thought she was walking in her sleep. I lay still, feeling that perhaps I was really dreaming. But when she wrapped a dark cloak round her and took up Nico in her arms, I began to get frightened. So I called to her softly, and at once she turned to me with a finger on her lips. "Hush," she said in a strange voice, very soft but quite dead and even. "Go to sleep, Hermione. I must go, but I can't leave Nicostratus. Sssh! Don't wake him . . . Go to sleep; I'll be back soon." Then she wrapped Nico in a soft lambskin and went out of the room. I thought father must have sent for her to Crete, or that grandfather Tyndareus was ill, or something like that. But still I felt strange and frightened.

'Everything was very quiet after she left the room, but I

could hear music in the distance. It was a pipe, but not an ordinary one that the shepherds play. At first I thought it must be Pan himself away up on the foothills of Taygetos, and that was why I felt frightened. But I know now that it was a Phrygian flute, playing the evil barbarian music from the cruel eastern lands where they serve Hecate and charm kind Selene the Moon Maiden down out of the sky into the dark caves of Latmos . . . In the morning I was woken by people shouting and running about the palace. Mother was gone, with Nico — and so was Paris the Trojan. Four of the guards lay dead; the treasury had been broken open and much gold stolen. We sent fast chariots on all the roads. Those who went to Gytheion returned in the evening to say that the Trojan ship had sailed before dawn and was almost out of sight towards the island of Cythera by the time they reached the shore.'

Hermione paused, and gazed out with troubled eyes over the wall and down the long valley to the wide plain of Argos with the glint of blue sea far away by Lerna, as if trying to see through the distance to where Paris the Trojan pirate had taken fair Helen on that spring morning six months before.

There was silence for a little while, broken only by the murmur of voices from the big citadel of Mycenae, and the soft notes of a shepherd's pipe far away on the hillside beyond the walls.

Then there was a patter of footsteps, and Kilissa, the nurse who attended on King Agamemnon's daughters, and who had once been a princess herself in a barbarian land in the south of Asia Minor before a Cretan pirate had captured her and sold her as a slave in rich Mycenae, came hastening from the palace and down the steps into the New Courtyard.

'Kilissa!' called Iphigeneia, 'we're up here on the watch-tower!'

'You have been a long time,' exclaimed Electra severely. 'And you've forgotten to bring a jug to fetch water in. That one cup won't be enough for all three of us. But of course if you like running up and down the ninety-three steps to the cistern —'

'Indeed, and there are always pots and to spare under yon wall, and you know it!' panted Kilissa in her sing-song Asiatic Greek as she toiled up the steep steps to the alcove above the wall where the three girls were sitting. 'And it's you yourself said you were going and fetching up the water.'

'I'll come with you, Kilissa,' cried Hermione eagerly. 'I've never seen your underground cistern, but I've heard about it! We've nothing like it at Sparta, though father says he would like to build one.'

Kilissa set the tray on the stone seat, and the evening sunlight flashed suddenly on the round gold cup with its pattern of wild bulls standing out in relief all over it.

'And it's glad I shall be for your help,' she said, smiling at Hermione. 'And we'd better be hurrying, and all. There are guests down in the Palace yard, and who they'll be I wasn't for knowing, but I heard the King bidding the slaves bring wine and fruit to this courtyard. So maybe he'll be sending you in when he comes.'

'I'm sure he'll let us stay if I ask him, and we're very quiet,' said Iphigeneia, while Hermione started down the steps, calling after her, 'Come along, Kilissa! We must get the cold, cold water from the bottom of the ninety-three steps.'

Down in the courtyard Hermione waited for Kilissa,

who led the way to the next corner where a pointed entrance beneath the wall led into the cistern.

At the bottom of the first flight of steps was a square platform where a rock-crystal lamp shaped like a duck stood burning on a ledge, and along the wall were ranged fat round earthenware jugs with narrow mouths decorated in red and black spirals.

Kilissa took the lamp by the duck's neck, which formed a handle, picked up a jug, and led the way down another dark staircase to the left, round another corner and then down the main flight of more than fifty steps until they saw the dark glimmer of water in front of them and stopped at the edge of the big stone cistern which was almost a small reservoir.

'The water comes in by the pipe up there,' Kilissa explained to Hermione as she filled the jug. 'When there is danger, indeed, the water is let in and comes half-way up these steps. It's plaster you'll be seeing on the walls to keep in the water.'

'Oh, what an exciting place!' cried Hermione, and her voice echoed strangely up the dark tunnel of the stairway. 'Father's often told me about it: he said it was one of the wonders of Mycenae. I expect King Atreus's great tomb is even more wonderful, but that would have made me feel sad, and this is only exciting.'

When they reached the last platform Kilissa turned to replace the lamp, and Hermione ran on up the final flight of steps and out into the bright sunshine and dark shadow of the courtyard.

Three men had just come down from the Palace, one King Agamemnon in his long robe of white, and the other two short tunicked and dusty as if from a journey by chariot. They had obviously left helmets and light

armour in the Palace, but stopped only to wash their hands and faces.

The nearer was a short, rather sturdy man of about thirty with dark hair and dark, thoughtful eyes. The other seemed younger, was tall and fair-haired with a handsome face, open and rather boyish . . .

'Oh!' shrieked Hermione. 'It's father!'

She rushed forward and a moment later Menelaus had caught her up in his arms and was kissing her, while she clung to him laughing and sobbing with excitement.

A little later Agamemnon and Menelaus had introduced their companion, young King Odysseus of Ithaca, and they were sitting with the three girls up on the watchtower.

'Shall I send the children away?' suggested Agamemnon. 'We've serious things to talk about, far above the heads of little girls like Electra and Hermione.'

'Oh please don't,' begged Hermione. 'I do want to know what's happened . . . Did you find mother and Nico? And have you got them back from those wicked Trojans?'

'I'm afraid not,' answered Menelaus sadly. 'I think Hermione ought to be told,' he added, turning to Agamemnon. 'But I don't know about my nieces.'

Electra flashed a dark look of anger at him, while Agamemnon rubbed his chin anxiously and hesitated.

'Let them hear,' said Odysseus briefly, but with a slight smile. 'Hermione should be told, and if she is, the other two won't give her a moment's peace until they worm it all out of her . . . Well, one of these young ladies certainly intends to do so, or I am much mistaken.'

Menelaus smiled too, but Electra tapped angrily with

her foot on the stone floor and bit viciously into her honey-cake.

'And so we give her up – or fight?' said Agamemnon, sipping his wine thoughtfully and looking across at Menelaus.

'Give her up?' exclaimed Menelaus hotly. 'There was never any talk of that! What about the oath we all swore?'

'But for the whole host of the Achaians, and most of the princes of Hellas – whether my vassals or not – to go to war with Phrygia over one woman,' said Agamemnon.

'It's more than that,' exclaimed Odysseus quickly, 'and you know it, High King of Mycenae. This war was bound to come, the war of the Greeks and the barbarians. We are all in, even without the oath, all of us who call our-selves Hellenes, whether we live in Greece or in the islands, whether we are vassals to Mycenae, or but spear-friends, or kings and princes of our own free islands, or states or cities. I suppose this struggle has been coming for a long time. The barbarians think we are weak and divided; they certainly grow stronger and stronger. It's not just the one main city of Troy that we must over-come; all the cities of Phrygia are their allies, and Priam is their overlord just as you, Agamemnon, are overlord of Achaia. And he has allies just as you have. It's to be Phrygia against Greece – East against West – however much we may pretend that it's only Mycenae against Troy: Agamemnon winning back his brother's wife from Paris the pirate. And this was their direct act of defiance. If we do not fight for Helen, who will be safe? Ship after ship of Troy will come to our coasts and carry off our wives and daughters. And soon they will be sacking our cities and taking our treasures, and our people as slaves.'

Odysseus paused, and Menelaus broke in, 'Well, why hesitate to fight? Atreus is dead and buried, and all the power is yours.'

Agamemnon nodded: 'While Atreus was living I might not have been able to call out all our vassals and allies to fight Troy – for Helen. Perhaps you are right, Odysseus. This war had to come. But I should have preferred to wait another few years. Although Atreus resigned the rule to me when he grew old, I have only just become High King in more than name ... But tell me what happened on your embassy to Troy?'

'Nothing happened,' said Menelaus shortly. 'They were most polite, the Trojans. Positively oily. There was one decent one, though, a man called Antenor, whose wife Theano, Queen Hecuba's sister, is the priestess of Athena.'

'You may well say so,' remarked Odysseus grimly. 'He saved our lives. Those wild beasts, the sons of King Priam, wanted to kill us out of hand, but Antenor got up and made a fine speech on the duties of hospitality and the anger of the gods at the murder of guests or ambassadors: it was a bit pompous, but I couldn't have done it better myself. Then Aeneas followed his example; he's the prince of a place near Troy called Lyrnessos, and is a cousin and ally of old Priam. After that they behaved better, and Hector, the Crown Prince, went so far as to apologize. He's quite decent, for a barbarian. And I think it was really all Paris's doing.'

'But didn't you demand the return of Helen and your son – to say nothing of the treasure?' asked Agamemnon, looking his haughtiest. 'What excuse, except barefaced war, could they offer? And there was no declaration of war: my brother received this Paris as a guest of noble family – one prince welcoming another.'

'They talked a lot of nonsense!' cried Menelaus angrily. 'Hesione had not been returned to them; Telamon had taken her by force, and refused to give her up. Absolute nonsense: Heracles won her fairly to begin with; and then he and Telamon and Peleus conquered Troy in open war when Priam's father King Laomedon was alive.'

'That was the excuse,' agreed Odysseus. 'The arguments were excellent, but they were all based on twisted facts. The point was simply that Paris had got Helen, and was not going to give her back. The Trojans seem to be quite mad about her, and even old Priam said it was worth fighting a war to keep her. I warned him that he'd lose both her and Troy; that if we fought it would be a long, bitter war which could only end when we had levelled Troy with the ground, killed all his sons and sold all his daughters into slavery. I also suggested (after I'd painted the grimmest picture I could of the horrors of war) that it was ridiculous to destroy Troy and kill the flower of their youth and ours for the sake of one woman. And I recommended the return of Helen, with a suitable fine and abject apologies.'

'Then his son, that scented barbarian pirate Paris, had the impudence to say that Helen came of her own free will – begged to be taken, in fact!' exploded Menelaus, upsetting his wine in his anger at the recollection of it. 'I told him exactly what I thought of him, and what any decent Greek would think of a man who behaved as he had done. They suggested murdering us after that, which I suppose is all one can expect of Trojans.'

'They're not all so bad,' remarked Odysseus thoughtfully. 'Our host was that Antenor, King Priam's brother-in-law and cousin, who saved us from those young hooligans of princes. They're a good, pious household: of course Theano is the head-priestess. They entertained us well and kindly, and Antenor openly expressed his disgust at Paris's behaviour and his disapproval of war over such a cause. They've several nice children, though they're older than any of you except Iphigeneia. Oh, there was one delightful little girl about four years old, but it turned out that she was Priam's youngest daughter, Polyxena, who more or less lived with them.'

'Of course, Antenor has been to Greece,' remarked Menelaus, 'and of all people he stayed with our — I mean your, namby-pamby vassal, young Palamedes down at Nauplia.'

'Perhaps that's where Palamedes gets his smooth, eastern ways,' remarked Odysseus. 'But then I'm biased against him, after that trick he played on me!'

'It was the action of a loyal man,' said Agamemnon severely. 'And it was a nice way of keeping the oath you yourself proposed, Odysseus — pretending to be so mad that you couldn't possibly come to help get back Helen.'

Odysseus smiled. 'I'd have come willingly enough,' he remarked, with a twinkle in his eye. 'I vowed to come, sane or mad, and I would have too — if you could have put up with my lunacy! Still, it was clever of Palamedes to catch me out as he did, and I suppose I ought to admire him for it ... But I knew it would be a long, dreary war, and Penelope and I were so happy in little Ithaca, particularly since my Telemachus was born.'

Odysseus sighed, and Iphigeneia asked timidly, 'Please, Uncle Menelaus, how did Palamedes prove that Odysseus wasn't really mad?'

Menelaus laughed. 'He fooled *me* completely,' he said. 'I can't tell you how grieved I was to see my best friend

28

ploughing the sand on the sea-shore with a cow and a donkey, harnessed to the plough, while he sowed salt in the furrows. However, when we were all watching the lunatic at work, and Penelope was weeping and wringing her hands, Palamedes suddenly snatched baby Telemachus from the nurse and placed him on the ground in front of the plough. Along came Odysseus with his head on one side, jibbering nonsense and slobbering at the mouth: but as soon as he saw Telemachus he forgot all about that as he guided the cow and the donkey across the newly sown furrows and rushed to snatch up the baby.'

'I only just managed to turn them in time,' admitted Odysseus. 'It was a near thing, and needed all my strength and judgement. I can't blame myself for forgetting about the madness, but I can blame Palamedes for risking the child's life – and I'll pay him out one of these days!'

'Palamedes is a good and useful captain,' said Agamemnon rather loftily, 'and we must have no quarrels among ourselves, Odysseus. He mayn't be quite the type Menelaus likes – or you either – but he's one of the cleverest men in Argolis. Look at that light-house he's built by the harbour at Nauplia: entirely his invention, nobody thought of light-houses to guide ships at night before he did. And he's working out a way of telling quantities of corn, or gold or anything by balancing it against specially prepared discs of metal which he calls weights. He can write our linear script better than any of my scribes, and he says there ought to be a new way of spelling words, using the sounds to make letters instead of syllables. I don't quite understand what he means, but that's what he said.'

'I know he's clever,' agreed Menelaus, 'but he's rather tiresome and effeminate. And I hate the way he's always praising people to their faces, and then saying unpleasant things about them behind their backs.'

'I don't know how we came to be talking about Palamedes,' remarked Odysseus. 'We were actually discussing something much more important: the Trojan situation. The long and the short of it is – war. We barely escaped with our lives: there is no chance of getting Helen back by peaceful means. It might be possible by guile – but I doubt if I could effect an escape for the child Nicostratus as well. So war is the only answer, and in fact the Trojans are collecting their allies and strengthening their walls. I did a little spying while I was about it, and I may tell you that it's going to be a difficult city to take. It's nearly as far from the sea-coast as Mycenae is – well, three miles at least, and rather flatter, with two widish rivers wandering about, and several citadels and small towns up in the mountains not far away. The sooner we set out the better . . .'

He looked inquiringly at Agamemnon, who answered slowly, 'All my vassals and allies, and the rest of the princes who swore the oath to Tyndareus when Helen was given in marriage, have been warned. It needs only the messenger to tell each of them that we mean war, for their fleets to assemble at Aulis. That boy Achilles, the son of Peleus, chose the place: he's to be admiral as he seems to know more about sailing a fleet than most of us.'

'So he ought,' interrupted Odysseus, 'if the stories are true. They say his mother's a sea-nymph!'

'They'll say anything,' grunted Agamemnon. 'But now let's consider the best way of dealing with these Trojans, destroying their city, getting Helen back and making sure that their power is broken once and for all. As far as I can calculate we may count on a good thousand ships, under thirty or forty leaders, with me of course as commander-in-chief by right of my position as High King of Mycenae and ruler of the Achaians. Even the Cretans have learnt their lesson, and Idomeneus will come: his schedule is eighty ships, though the last lists gave him nearer a hundred. If we sail by way of the islands of Scyros, Lemnos and Tenedos, we shall —'

Agamemnon was launching out into a long and pompous plan for the invasion of Troy, but he was interrupted by his small niece Hermione who burst suddenly into loud weeping.

'Oh, oh!' she sobbed, burying her face against Menelaus's arm. 'You go on and on about Troy, and the war, and all these men who are going to fight — but you've said nothing about mother, and dear little Nico. Aren't they coming back? Didn't you even see them? What did mother say? Oh, I want her back, I want her, I want her!'

Menelaus took her on his knee and tried his best to comfort her, while Agamemnon, after looking annoyed and put out for a minute or two, shrugged his shoulders and smiled rather weakly at his two daughters who had been listening eagerly to all that had been said.

'No, dear,' Menelaus replied to Hermione's questions when her sobs had calmed down a little. 'They wouldn't even let me see Helen — nor Nicostratus. They said she had gone willingly with Paris ... But I can't believe it. It's not true; I know it isn't.'

'No, it isn't true!' cried Hermione indignantly. 'I saw her go, and I know! She was drugged; she was walking in a dream; that evil Trojan pipe had taken away her wits, just as Pan takes away the wits of the shepherds

31

Chapter 1

POLYXENA'S BRACELET

Nicostratus always felt certain that he could remember Sparta. His earliest recollection was of giant mountains towering above him, up and up into a dark sky against which they gleamed cold and white. Then he remembered the tossing of a ship, with the foam splashing over the side and a red sail flapping above his head.

'You have seen ships since we came to Troy,' said Helen when he told her. 'But you have never been near mountains. Ida over there in the distance is the only mountain you've seen in Phrygia ... Yes, it is Sparta that you remember ... Taygetos in the moonlight – on that terrible, terrible night when the madness came upon me – yes, it was there above us, so cold and beautiful. It seemed to be reproaching me.'

Helen sobbed suddenly, and Nicostratus snuggled up to her quickly.

'I'm sorry, mother dear,' he said softly. 'I didn't mean to remind you of – of things that make you sad. But I do so want to remember Sparta, to remember that I haven't always been a prisoner in Troy. And being on the sea must have been when we were coming here too, mustn't it? Of course we can see the ships from here, but they're so far away! And Greece is over the water, isn't it?'

'Yes, Nico, it's very far away,' sighed Helen, but she smiled too as she put her arm round his shoulders and looked out over the wide plain of Troy to the blue gleam of the sea nearly three miles away.

In the clear evening light they could see the Greek ships drawn up on the shore behind their low wall, and the Greek huts, thatched with rushes, in front of them making a small town of low wooden buildings behind a palisade of pointed stakes which had stood there so long that some of the pine-trunks had taken root and sent out shoots of green.

Over the sand-dunes beyond the Scamander River to the west, the open sea was also visible, with the island of Tenedos glowing rosy as the low clouds behind it caught the first flush of sunset.

'We weren't always prisoners in Troy,' said Helen, looking back over the long, dreary space of nearly ten years since Paris had come to Sparta.

'But we were on the sea for many, many days before we reached here, and you may well remember something of our voyage . . . We went to Cythera first — the island one can just see from Gytheion. But we only stayed there one night. After that a terrible storm arose: I thought it was the angry breath of the gods, and that we should be dashed on the rocks or swallowed up by the sea at any moment. But after many nights and days we came to Cyprus, where we stayed for a long time. There more Trojan ships joined us, and Paris went off with several of them to Sidon. I prayed that he might not return, but he came for us with his ships laden with spoil. After that we sailed north round the coast of Phrygia and among the islands — Rhodos, Kos, Patmos, Samos, Chios, Lesbos, Tenedos, the bright jewels of the Aegean — until we came to the Hellespont over there and turned into the mouth of the Scamander . . . Then I saw

Troy for the first time: the town and the citadel, the high walls and this tall tower – our prison for these long, long years . . . And still no end to it.'

Nicostratus stirred uncomfortably. Although he was so anxious to remember Sparta, to prove to himself that he was a Greek and not a Trojan, he had grown up in Troy, he knew no other life. Sometimes he liked to tell himself firmly that he was a Greek, and different from the Trojans; but that was usually when he had been teased or bullied by the other children in Troy. This did not happen very often when he was small, for the war had not drawn close to Troy, and there was much talk among the princes of 'driving the Greeks out in the spring, or burning their ships and making slaves of those who were not killed'.

But as year after year went by and the Greeks sacked and burnt city after city in the hills round about, and drew nearer and nearer to Troy itself, the tone began to change.

Prince Paris, who had seldom shown his dislike for Nicostratus, could not now see him without muttering some cruel taunt or unkind remark; and one day Nico came running up to Helen's tower bruised and bleeding, chased by a gang of Trojan children shouting, 'Greek traitor! foreign spy!'

After this Nicostratus did not venture down into the city, but spent his time in the citadel. At first he was usually with Helen in the tower; but as Paris became more unkind, he began to spend longer and longer in the house of Antenor, near the Temple of Pallas Athena in the middle of the citadel.

With Antenor and his wife, the priestess Theano, Nicostratus found peace and kindness. And sometimes Helen

35

would come to the house also and sit there quietly with her embroidery talking to Theano, or more often in silence, watching the children at their play.

For at Antenor's house Nicostratus found a companion and friend in the young princess Polyxena, King Priam's youngest child, who was barely two years older than he was himself. Polyxena lived with Antenor and Theano, partly because Priam wished her to become a priestess of Athena, and partly because she, too, felt lonely and out of place in her own home.

'Now that all my sisters are married,' she told Nicostratus, 'the palace is full of shouting men. That's the worst of having so many brothers! It wasn't so bad before Troilus was killed, he was only a few years older than I am. Of course Polydorus is the same age as you are; but now that father has sent him away for safety to be looked after by my sister Ilione and her husband over in Thrace, there's not even anyone near my own age . . . I don't want to be a priestess: one in the family's enough, and we've got Cassandra, who's one too many as it is! But it's quiet and peaceful here: Theano's a bit strict, but old Antenor's such a dear. And it's fun having you. Of course you're really a Greek, and the Greeks are the hated enemies of Troy; but somehow you're different.'

So the two grew up together, and Antenor treated them just as if they were his own children.

'We owe young Nico a happy childhood at least,' he said to his wife. 'What Paris did was altogether evil, and no good can come of it. I told Priam and the princes so at the beginning when Menelaus and Odysseus came as envoys, and I tell them so whenever I get the chance: unless Helen is returned to her husband, and due fines paid by us, Troy will fall . . . And if Troy falls, Polyxena will be taken as a slave by one of the Greek kings: so *she* must have the happiest childhood we can give her, too.'

He and Theano did their best to live up to these high principles, and Nicostratus was happy – nearly all the time. But with them and Polyxena he found it harder and harder to remember the difference between Greeks and Trojans, just as she tended sometimes to forget that all Greeks were wicked invaders and that she ought to hate them.

It was only when he was with Helen that Nico remembered who and what he was, and could hate the Trojans. It worried him to see how sad and listless she was becoming, and it troubled him to see how her fear and dislike of Paris grew and grew, and how Paris took advantage of it more and more to make her life a misery.

As his home had become so unhappy, Nicostratus tended to run away from his troubles there whenever possible, and so he visited Helen less and less frequently. She had, however, sent for him on the day when he sat by her side on the tower-top looking out towards the Greek huts and the sea beyond, and talking of Greece itself.

'Something will happen soon,' said Helen presently. 'Lyrnessos was destroyed last month: that's the last city to stand out against the Greeks. It's Troy next. You've seen how they've been gathering in all their forces to prepare for the grand attack ... Oh, I hope it will be over soon!'

Next morning it seemed that Helen's wish was likely to come true. For at sunrise great bands of Greeks came marching over the plain towards Troy, with numerous chariots racing ahead of them. Over the branch of the Scamander they came – a dry hollow of smooth stones

37

now, but in winter a deep river flowing into the smaller stream of the Simois — and drew up just out of arrow-shot below the walls.

Both Nico and Polyxena sat with Helen on the tower that morning, and Nico felt a strange glow of pride and excitement as he looked down upon the tall warriors — his people — with their flashing bronze helmets and shields, who sped up and down in their chariots, standing up tall and grim, while their charioteers bent forward over the front, guiding the horses.

'That must be Ajax, the big man with the round shield,' said Helen, her voice shaking a little. 'And — oh, there's Odysseus: rather short, dark-haired . . . I remember him at Sparta when I was a girl. Look! That's Agamemnon, with the sceptre instead of a spear.'

'Who's the young man driving so recklessly — straight towards us?' asked Polyxena.

Helen shaded her eyes with her hand. 'I don't know,' she said at last.

'I think it's Achilles, their — our chief warrior,' said Nico a little uncertainly. 'I heard Hector talking about him, and he described him very well.'

Polyxena leant over the parapet as the chariot flashed by just below, and she flushed suddenly as the tall, power-fully-built young man shook back his golden hair and she saw his face for a moment.

'Oh!' Helen gave a little cry and her fingers grew white as she grasped the stone coping. 'There's Menelaus — my husband!'

Nico swung round eagerly from watching Achilles speed past the walls, but all he saw was a tall man in a chariot whose back was already towards him.

'The attack will come tomorrow,' said Helen with con-

viction. But although little camps were formed at various strategic places near Troy, and day by day chariots were to be seen patrolling the plain, no attack developed.

At last spies brought in word that many of the Greeks were suffering from a plague which had fallen on the camp; and although they were recovering, a quarrel had broken out between Achilles and Agamemnon.

The next report was that Achilles had withdrawn to his own camp beyond the main stream of the Scamander, with his cousin Patroclus and all their men, and refused to take further part in the war.

'At last!' said Paris, rubbing his hands and smiling. 'This is the chance we've been waiting for! Tomorrow we attack them—keeping well away from Achilles and his army—break them and burn the ships before this quarrel is patched up . . . Hector will lead the attack, of course. And I'll see if we can get a private message through to Achilles offering a separate peace with him. We might even pay him to go away!'

'Yes,' said Helen cuttingly, 'and then waylay him and get back the bribe, I suppose.'

'By Zeus, that's a good idea!' exclaimed Paris, quite seriously. 'I must go and have a word with Hector and Pandarus about it.'

'Hector will have none of such vile tricks,' cried Helen indignantly. 'He's almost the only one of you who isn't a complete barbarian. As for Pandarus, he's as ready for any mean trick as – as you are yourself.'

'You Greeks don't understand war,' sneered Paris contemptuously. 'I suppose you'd expect us to send a herald to Agamemnon saying that we quite understand his difficulties, and wouldn't dream of attacking until Achilles had stopped sulking and come to heel again!

As for our ally Pandarus, Prince of Zelea, he's a sensible fighting man, just as I am — and as all we Phrygians are — and not one of Agamemnon's honourable idiots.'

Nevertheless, next day when the Trojan forces moved out against the Greeks, the whole war came near to ending in a strictly honourable single combat.

For as the Trojans, shouting threats and war-cries, marched out towards the silent ranks of the Greeks, Paris, with his panther-skin over his shoulder and waving two spears at once, in a rash moment of boastfulness challenged any of the Greek princes to come and fight him, man to man, in a duel to the death.

Menelaus heard this, and springing from his chariot, in full armour as he was, strode out towards him, shouting, 'Now at last, coward and thief, I can take my revenge on you!' This was more than Paris had bargained for, and he was slinking hastily away behind the Trojan archers when Hector, who had heard and seen all, caught him by the shoulder and stopped him.

'Paris, you wretch!' he exclaimed. 'You cowardly cheat! You can steal women, but you daren't fight men; and you make us a scorn to the Greeks, who think we choose our leaders for their pretty faces. Now that you've challenged Menelaus, you shall fight him in single combat — and perhaps we can end the war here and now at a blow, as I wish we had done nine years ago.'

Then he turned and motioned to his men to stop their advance, holding up his spear by the middle as a signal for a truce.

So the duel took place, after a solemn swearing of oaths that the winner should have Helen and pay a fine, and that the truce would be respected and the war ended by the death of either Menelaus or Paris.

They cast lots, and Paris threw his spear first, but it failed to pierce Menelaus's shield. Menelaus, however, sent his spear through Paris's shield, and the armour beneath, but to one side so that it only grazed his hip. Then he rushed forward and struck at Paris, breaking his own sword into several pieces but half stunning him.

With a cry of triumph Menelaus caught Paris by the big horse-hair crest on his helmet, and dragged him away towards the Greek lines. To reach them he was forced to cross the almost dry bed of the side-stream of the Scamander, and while pulling him up the further bank the straps of the helmet broke, and Menelaus fell backwards, while Paris rolled down into the reeds which fringed the water-course.

Menelaus picked himself up and plunged down into the reeds. But Paris had disappeared, and at length he came up on to his own bank, very hot and angry, vowing that Aphrodite must have carried Paris away.

'He's a coward, like most of these barbarians,' shouted Agamemnon. 'But never mind him. You won the battle, and so the Trojans must give Helen up to you!'

Menelaus therefore stood up and called to the Trojans, 'Prince Hector, your cowardly brother has escaped somehow. But you saw that I defeated him. So, according to your solemn oaths, you must give up Helen to me, and pay a suitable fine for all the evil he has done to us.'

'King Menelaus,' answered Hector, 'you are in the right. And indeed, if I had had my way, you and Odysseus would have taken both Helen and the fine when you came to Troy more than nine years ago.'

But Pandarus, the crafty king of Zelea, Priam's ally and Paris's closest friend, drew an arrow from his quiver, fitted it to his bow, and loosed it suddenly at Menelaus, wounding him in the thigh.

After this the battle broke in earnest, and the fighting surged backwards and forwards all that day, and for many days to come.

As for Paris, he appeared inside Troy without his helmet, but smiling grimly, walking quietly from the Temple of Athena not long after his strange disappearance.

'I'm not as fortunate with Menelaus as I was with his wife,' he remarked casually to Helen. 'I always said that Greeks should be shot with bows and arrows like other vermin. I wish Pandarus had aimed a little better!'

Paris did not venture down on to the plain of Troy for some time after this – not until the Trojans had driven the Greeks right down to the sea-coast and were camping just outside their stockade. He was back again in Troy not long afterwards, however, declaring that it was unsafe to sleep out in the open with Greeks about. This was after Odysseus and Diomedes had stolen into the Trojan camp by night, killed the newly arrived King Rhesus of Thrace, and driven off his beautiful white horses.

But next day Hector made a breach in the Greek stockade, wounded Odysseus and set fire to several of the ships. Now, however, the tide of battle turned. For Patroclus appeared suddenly, wearing his cousin Achilles's armour and leading his men: and the Trojans fled, thinking that it was Achilles himself.

Hector, however, killed Patroclus and only with great difficulty did the giant Ajax manage to carry off the body, not before Hector had stripped it of the beautiful armour of Achilles.

There was joy in Troy that night, and Paris strutted about boasting that the war was nearly over.

'You sound as if you had killed Patroclus yourself,' said Helen bitterly. 'But while you sit here drinking and bragging, Hector, who did slay him, is out on the plain. And tomorrow I very much fear that Achilles in his anger will be more than a match even for noble Hector.'

Helen's words proved only too true. Next day Achilles, almost frantic with grief and rage, led the united Greek forces against the Trojans. From the tower Helen and Nicostratus could see most of the battle, and never for a moment did they lose sight of Achilles, whose new armour of gleaming bronze flashed and shone in the sunlight until he seemed to be clothed in fire.

At last Hector fell, and Achilles stripped the body, tied it to the back of his chariot, and drove in triumph round the walls of Troy.

Helen wept at the sight. 'Poor Hector,' she sobbed. 'He alone of all the Trojans has treated me as a Greek prince would have done. Never in all these long, bitter years did he speak a harsh word to me or show me anything but gentleness and courtesy. Now we are truly alone and undefended. Oh, Artemis, you who guide Sparta and the whole of lovely Lacedaimon, may the end come quickly!'

Next day there was great activity out on the plain for the funeral of Patroclus, and Nico and Polyxena sat on the tower straining their eyes to see what was happening, while Helen tried to explain it to them.

'That great pile of wood they're building is to burn the body,' she said. 'And as he was so great a hero and the Prince of Opos, there'll be a sacrifice of animals, as well as wine and honey.'

'But I thought that you – we – in Greece were buried in tombs,' said Nico, to whom Helen had often described the great bee-hive tombs of Mycenae, and the one which Menelaus had started to build at Sparta.

'That's only for those who die in peace,' explained Helen. 'It's an honour to be killed in war, and so the flesh is destroyed quickly by fire, and then the spirit is free to pass into the kingdom of Hades, Lord of the Dead. For those who are buried in tombs there is the long wandering of the spirit, while the flesh decays. That's what the tombs are for: the spirit must still return to the flesh from time to time, and taste the offerings of wine and cakes and honey left in the tomb. But once the flesh has gone, the spirit is safe with Hades, and we sweep aside the useless bones and place the next body safely where they lay in the tomb. So you see, by tomorrow the spirit of Patroclus will be free to enter the Land of the Dead, for there will only be charred bones left. That, as I said, is the reward of those who die bravely in battle ... And anyhow the battlefield is hardly the place to build or dig tombs of stone and rock – and most battles are fought far away from home.'

'Then it won't matter if Hector's body is left unburied and unburnt as Achilles threatens?' asked Nico doubtfully.

'That's different!' exclaimed Polyxena quickly. 'It's an insult to the gods, in Phrygia as well as in Greece, and keeps the spirit for ever out of the land of the Dead, until the bones turn at last into dust. He must be burnt or buried ... Oh my poor, dear brother Hector! How I wish this horrible war would stop!'

Polyxena burst into tears, and Helen comforted her as best she could, while Nico watched the distant Greeks with a strange fascination, until a cloud of smoke from the newly lighted pyre swirled down and hid them from view.

45

The fire burnt fiercely far into the night, and next day the watchers on the walls of Troy saw the great Funeral Games held to do honour to the dead hero of the Greeks.

The dead hero of Troy was, however, still unburied, and Achilles continued to drag his body round the city twice daily and returned only angry and offensive answers to the heralds whom Priam sent to offer ransom for his son's body. At last the old king took matters into his own hands and left Troy one night in his chariot, accompanied only by his charioteer. He returned before the morning and told in glowing terms how he had been received by Achilles and had won him over by reminding him of his own old father, King Peleus.

'A sentimental fool – like all Greeks,' was Paris's comment. 'And it was sheer madness on father's part to take the risk. If Achilles hadn't been such a fool, he'd have captured him there and then, and who knows whether our people wouldn't have been weak enough to exchange you against him. Not that I would have let you go . . . As it is, he's got back Hector's body, but only in exchange for his weight in gold. I doubt if we've enough left in all Troy; and if we have, it's a ridiculous waste to give it all for a mere dead body . . . In fact I shall try and stop it. Now that Hector's dead, I'm the eldest son, and the heir to the throne. I wish our kings retired as yours do in Greece when they're too old to rule any more: it's the only good Greek custom I've ever come across – except for leaving their wives unguarded like that ridiculous husband of yours.'

With this final gibe Paris went swaggering off to the council and left Helen with her eyes flashing, too angry to find anything to say.

Paris's irreligious suggestion did not find favour with the Trojan princes and warlords. Indeed he had hardly begun to make it when old Antenor sprang up in his place and cried, 'Cease from your blasphemies, Prince Paris: do not add further to the load of guilt that you have brought upon Troy. If war there had to be between Greece and Phrygia, could we not have gone to war honestly? Could we not have said: "The passage through the Hellespont to trade with Colchis and Tauris and the other ports of the Black Sea is ours, and if you do not respect our rights, we fight!" Why must you go as a peaceful visitor to Sparta and there flout the sacred duties of hospitality, the divine bond of honour between host and guest, by carrying off the wife of your host and robbing him of his treasure as well? Oh, be sure a curse is upon us for that action! Do not bring an even greater curse upon us from the gods by leaving brave Hector unburied – to save gold, forsooth!'

'All that antiquated nonsense is out of date!' began Paris angrily. 'It's high time old men like you, yes, and my father King Priam too, left young men to manage this war. And many other things too. Hector would never have been killed if you'd done as I suggested, and that long-haired lout Achilles would have been bribed – or, better still, put out of the way, by poison if necessary –'

'Paris!' the one word silenced him as Priam spoke it, and he sank back on to his seat while the old king continued in a voice still full and strong, and in the rolling words which came so naturally to his generation. 'Speak such thoughts again, and by our father Zeus and our lady Aphrodite, I'll hand you over bound to King Menelaus, and Helen with you: yes, and all the treasure you stole. Oh, how truly your mother dreamt on the night of your

47

birth that her child was a firebrand who would consume all Troy!'

So it was agreed to ransom Hector's body for its weight in gold, and next morning Idaius the herald went out of Troy to carry the message to Achilles and the Greeks.

Before noon Achilles and the majority of the Greek princes, with a large guard of foot-soldiers, arrived in front of Troy at the place where the wall was lowest and ran straight down to the rock which there lay level in a small shelf before sloping away into the plain. Round the rest of Troy the walls slanted up the steep slope before rising perpendicularly, or else were built, like Helen's tower, on the edge of a low cliff that rose from the marshy ground which ran along the lesser stream of the Scamander to its joining with the Simois.

Immediately below the wall Achilles caused a great pair of scales to be made and set up; and this was carried out quickly and skilfully under the direction of Palamedes, the prince of Nauplia, who was famous for his mechanical skill and his various inventions.

Nicostratus and Polyxena were on the wall early, eager to see all there was to be seen.

'Most of the Greek leaders will be there, I expect,' said Nico. 'We'll be able to see them from quite close. I want to be able to recognize them all.'

But really it was to see Menelaus that he had made a point of getting the best place on the wall – the father whom he could not really remember, and had seen only as a distant figure far away upon the plain of Troy.

'Achilles will be there,' murmured Polyxena, half to herself, and she flushed suddenly as she thought of the young demi-god with golden hair and golden armour who had flashed past in his chariot.

48

Helen came too: but Paris ordered her back to her tower with sneers and gibes that made Nico feel desperately for the sword that he was not allowed to carry, and plan over and over again just where he would strike with it.

Menelaus did not come to the weighing, however, though Agamemnon was there, accompanied by old Nestor his councillor, the most ancient of all the Greek leaders. Odysseus was there also, and the gigantic Ajax; but few others, besides Palamedes and some of the younger chiefs.

When the two uprights had been driven into a crevice in the rock, the round log lashed across the top of them, and the long beam tied more loosely across this, like a see-saw, Palamedes hung long flat boards, each by four ropes fastened to their corners, at either end. Then he climbed up on to the rounded log and adjusted the beam until both sides balanced exactly. Then, having driven in six small metal wedges – two either side of the beam, and one in each side of it between them, to prevent it from slipping – he sprang lightly to the ground and shouted to Talthybius, the Greek herald, 'There now, all's weady! Tell Achilles to come and bwing the body!' Then he turned towards the wall, and called up to Priam in the same high, lisping voice: 'King of Twoy, the scales are fair to a hair's bweadth: so pile your gold in the side neawest to you!'

'I don't think much of Prince Palamedes,' muttered Nico. 'I hate the way he talks, and he doesn't look as if he would be much good in battle. Of course height isn't everything – Odysseus is no taller than he is – but he just doesn't look like a warrior at all.'

'No,' said Polyxena, her voice trembling a little, 'but

here comes one who does . . . A prince who looks like one of the gods themselves!'

As she spoke Achilles appeared over the edge of the little plateau and strode up to the farther end of the scales. He was in shining armour, but wore no helmet; his golden hair hung almost to his shoulders, and his frank boyish face made him appear almost too young to be the best and most skilful fighting man in the whole Greek army.

Behind him four men carried the body of Hector, now decently washed and wrapped in fine purple linen soaked with perfume. They laid him reverently in the scale farthest from Troy, at a word from Palamedes continuing to take the weight so that it should not sink right to the ground.

Then out from the Skaian Gate of Troy came old Priam on foot, with Aeneas and Antenor accompanying him, and behind them a led chariot piled with bags of gold. They took their stand beside the scale nearest to Troy, and at a word from Priam the attendants opened the bags and began to arrange bars and ingots of gold on the broad piece of wood to balance Hector.

At last the bags were empty, and the bearers stepped back from the body, while all eyes turned to the beam which now rocked gently on the rounded wood.

'Hector still sinks lower than the gold,' said Achilles in his strong, clear voice. 'A few more ounces will more than balance him. I hate to seem a mere chaffering merchant, King Priam, but as I told you I am bound by oath not to give up Hector's body for less than his weight in gold.'

'Alas,' exclaimed Priam, 'I have no more! My Treasury is empty!'

'Fool!' spluttered Paris under his breath. 'He'll be telling them how low our food supplies are next!'

There was a moment of awkward silence, and then with a sudden exclamation, Polyxena leant forward over the edge of the wall.

'As Hector's youngest sister I add my share to the ransom!' she cried; and she flung down into the scale beneath her first her heavy gold ear-rings, then her gold necklace and lastly the great gold bracelet which was clasped about her left wrist.

Slowly the scale sank, until all could see that Hector's body hung a foot or more higher from the ground than the pile of gold against which it was balanced.

'I accept the ransom!' cried Achilles. 'Take Hector's body, and give it honourable burial in whatever way the customs of Troy may demand. And take also the gold: I give it as a present to the father of the noblest and bravest man whom it has ever been my lot to stand against in battle, and to slay in fair fight. Never let it be said that Achilles, son of Peleus, bought and sold the bodies of his enemies . . . As ransom for Hector I take only this!'

So saying he took from the scale the golden bracelet and clasped it round his wrist.

'Fair Princess Polyxena!' he cried, 'I wear this in honour of your brother, and of your action in casting down your adornments to ransom him. I would the gods had given me a sister to do the like for me!'

Then their eyes met, and Achilles became suddenly silent, his lips parted as if in wonder. And he seemed to be walking in a dream as he turned to acknowledge Priam's thanks, before striding away with the rest of the Greeks towards their camp by the sea-shore.

Chapter 2

UNDER WHICH KING?

After the ransoming of Hector, Polyxena also seemed to be living in a dream, and Nicostratus found her suddenly a very dull companion. She seemed to have changed too, and was oddly distant, and no longer interested in the things which had been their main concern until now.

'She's grown up suddenly,' said Helen, when Nico complained of the unexpected loss of his one companion. 'Remember, she's fourteen ... You're getting on for manhood yourself!'

Helen sighed, and looked out over the plain towards the distant sea and the ships and the big stockade. She did not need to look so far for the Greeks now, for since the death of Hector they were beleaguering Troy more and more closely, and were encamped all round the city, with rough earth-works and palisades and log-huts. Guards marched up and down between each encampment, and it needed a pitched battle for any supplies or reinforcements to get into Troy; and even for the odd spy to slip in or out of the city was now a dangerous enterprise.

Nicostratus looked down at the Greeks too; and then he gazed back into Troy where the walls and towers were all manned by anxious watchers, and in the court-yard of the citadel and the streets and squares of the lower city groups gathered and dispersed, all talking in low, anxious tones. Suddenly he felt afraid, and very lost and strange: it was his home, yet not his home – he had no place in it, yet he could not imagine a place for himself anywhere else. To be grown-up was to be responsible, to think and act for himself: but still his mind went numb at the idea.

Helen saw his trouble, and put her arm round him, smiling gently, while the red Star Stone which she had worn on her breast ever since she came to Troy rose and fell as she sighed deeply.

'No,' she said, 'not yet. But the time will come, may come at any moment, when we shall have to decide – and act . . . Oh, Nico, what is going to become of us when Troy falls? Will Menelaus forgive me – can the Greeks allow him to forgive me? Think how many have died in this war – all because of me. Whether it was my fault or not, it was all because of me! Oh, it would have been better, far better if I had never been born!'

Now it was Nico's turn to comfort Helen – and she had never broken down so completely before, at least not in his presence. The red Star Stone shook and trembled until, in the fierce sunlight, the flash and glint of it seemed like red drops of blood falling on Helen's white dress and leaving no stain.

'Surely there's nothing to forgive!' exclaimed Nico. 'You couldn't help being carried off by Paris. Father shouldn't have left you unprotected when he went to Crete. And he and the Greeks wouldn't have fought this great war for your sake if they had not known that you were innocent.'

'The war had to come,' murmured Helen, remembering talks between Menelaus and Agamemnon on visits to Sparta or Mycenae. 'I'm only the pretext . . . But do you think the Trojans will let us be taken back in safety? Paris would kill me rather than know that I was with

Menelaus again. And even if Paris were dead, would not you and I be valuable hostages? . . . And, whatever Menelaus wants, might not the rest of the Greeks sacrifice such hostages in their determination to destroy the Trojans? . . . I tell you, Nico, we are in very great danger, and that danger grows greater every day. Now that Hector is dead, we have no protector.'

'What about Antenor?' asked Nico.

'Yes, he's a good and an honourable man,' said Helen, 'but he's old, and who will listen to him? Or even to Theano, though she is the high-priestess of Pallas Athena and guardian of the Luck of Troy. Why, no one pays any heed to Cassandra, Apollo's priestess — and you'd have thought that, being Priam's eldest daughter as well, her warnings would have been heeded above those of all other priestesses.'

This new sense of danger gave Nico much to think about, and with it came a feeling of excitement that was not altogether unpleasant.

'But what will happen next?' he asked.

'I don't know!' exclaimed Helen, clasping her hands. 'What does this strange waiting mean? Why don't the Greeks attack Troy? Priam's last allies, the Amazons, were defeated a week ago, and their queen, Penthesilia, killed by Achilles, but no move is made . . . Why? Why?'

'Has Priam no more allies?' asked Nico.

'There's his nephew, Memnon, who is called Prince of the Morning,' said Helen. 'He's the last of them, and Priam has sent envoys to beg him to come with as big an army of his black warriors as he can collect. It shows how desperate Priam is that he's sent as a gift to Memnon — or a bribe if you like — the most precious treasure in Troy.'

'What's that?' asked Nico. 'Surely not the Palladion?'

'Oh no,' laughed Helen. 'Priam wouldn't part with the Luck of Troy for anything. And no one would be pleased to get it either – a mere lump of black stone. No, he's sent Memnon the Golden Vine, which really is precious. Why, it has clusters of jewels instead of grapes, and the stems and leaves are made out of solid gold. He wouldn't have given that even to ransom Hector's body.'

'But the Palladion is surely more precious?' said Nico. 'Theano told Polyxena all about it, and she told me. It's the little black stone image of Pallas Athena which fell from heaven right on the spot where it stands in the kella of the Temple . . . The very Temple was built round it. And the city in which it stands can never be conquered.'

'Indeed,' murmured Helen, as if half doubting what Nico said. 'Well, you'd better carry it away to Menelaus and make our peace with the Greeks by getting it out of Troy.'

'Do you think they know about it?' asked Nico.

'They're sure to, if it's really as important as you say,' answered Helen. 'Calchas will have told them all about it. He's a Trojan, you know.'

'Who's Calchas?' asked Nico.

'He's a famous prophet or seer,' answered Helen. 'After the Trojans decided not to give me back, Priam sent Calchas to the great oracle of Apollo at Delphi – and he never came back to Troy. But it seems that he joined Agamemnon, and is now chief seer to the Greeks instead. It's said that the oracle at Delphi foretold the certain destruction of Troy and commanded Calchas to join the Greeks and stop them giving up the war, however long Troy took to fall. Later on Calchas prophesied that it would fall in the tenth year . . . We're in the tenth year now, so we shall see. Of course Paris says it's all lies put about by the Greeks to stop the Trojan allies from coming to Priam's aid. But Paris is such a liar himself, that I — well, I hope Calchas is right.'

'I couldn't steal the Palladion,' said Nico, shivering a little. 'Theano guards it so carefully. And — and it would bring a curse on anyone else who even touched it.'

'I'd risk the curse then — if I believed in the Palladion!' murmured Helen. 'But I wonder why the Greeks haven't attacked!'

As it happened, Helen was not to be left long in doubt. That very day there came an envoy from the Greeks with a message for Priam and his most trusted advisers — not a message even for the general council of the Trojans. As this embassy was so secret, the messenger was sent to Antenor's house, and there Priam came with two or three ancient councillors such as Anchises, the father of Aeneas. But Paris was there also, and this being so Antenor insisted that Helen must be present too.

Nicostratus came as well, but Paris told him brusquely to go away when he saw him coming up the steps at the side of the Temple. So he went down again, raging against Paris in his heart, and wishing even more desperately that he could slip into Antenor's room un-observed to hear what was going on.

As he turned the corner of the Temple he saw Polyxena standing in the shadow of one of the pillars, gazing eagerly up the staircase.

'An envoy from the Greeks?' she said, with a little gasp in her breath. 'It's Palamedes, who has been here before. He's the one who made the scales for weighing Hector's body, and he was standing by Achilles when I threw down my bracelet.'

'It's so secret a message that only Priam and Antenor and Anchises are to meet him,' said Nico. 'And Paris, of course. Antenor insisted on my mother coming too. I wanted to be there, but Paris chased me out.'

'Perhaps it's a peace offer — if you and Helen are handed over,' exclaimed Polyxena. 'You have a right to be there . . . I know a secret place from which we can see and hear all that happens in the room at the back of the Temple, which I expect is where they've gone. I was afraid to go there alone; and anyhow I don't think I could get up to it. But if you come with me —'

'Of course!' interrupted Nico eagerly. 'Show me the way, quickly!'

Polyxena turned at once and ran into the Temple. In the big, dim outer room, or 'kella', a single lamp burnt dimly on the altar in front of the low, narrow entrance to the inner shrine. Polyxena tiptoed past the lamp and slipped through into the darkness beyond.

'Mind where you put your feet,' she whispered, 'there's some sort of drain at the back of the altar which is used when sacrifices are made. It's a big stone with long slits in it: you can't fall through, but you might catch your foot in one of the slits.'

Treading warily, Nico followed her through the narrow entrance into the shrine which was almost completely dark. Once inside she took his hand and led him straight across the open floor.

'Slowly — and quietly,' she whispered, her voice trembling almost as much as the hand which Nico held. 'Oh, I hope no one comes — and that Pallas Athena will forgive us for desecrating her sanctuary like this! . . . Oh!' she gave a stifled cry. 'I've touched it — the

57

Palladion itself – on which only the hands of the priestess must ever rest!'

Polyxena was shivering all over when at last Nico drew close to her as she stopped against the farther wall. Looking back he could see the dim outline of the sacred image, the Palladion, between him and the narrow doorway to the outer room where the lamp flickered smokily; and far away through the outer door of the Temple and the double row of pillars in front of it he caught a glimpse of sunlight which seemed blindingly white by contrast.

'Where now?' he whispered.

'There's a ledge above our heads,' replied Polyxena in the same tone, 'you can just reach it, I think. If you can, scramble up quietly, and give me a hand when you get there.'

Nico did as he was told, and being an excellent climber he was soon lying on a kind of stone shelf a foot or more wide and reaching down to help Polyxena up.

When she was safely there, she led him along the ledge towards one of the side walls. In the very corner a roughly shaped tree-trunk supported the ceiling, and into it pegs were driven to form a kind of ladder.

Polyxena led the way up this, and through a small square hole in the corner of the wooden ceiling, into the triangularly-shaped roof-space which ran the whole length of the Temple and of the rooms beyond. The end wall of the Temple was built up in the middle to support the main central beam of the roof, but the stones sloped down jaggedly on either side, and it was easy to step over on to the ceiling of the room beyond. It was no longer quite dark, since a certain amount of light came up under the eaves on either side.

As soon as they had crossed the wall, Nico and Polyxena could hear voices speaking below them: and by lying down between the joists they could see quite easily through cracks or knot-holes in the rough boards into the first-floor room beneath. This room was lit by windows on either side, and was built above the treasury which formed the ground floor of the Temple beyond the shrine.

Priam was seated in Antenor's chair at the head of a table, with Anchises and Antenor on either side of him. Paris sat on the same side as Antenor, looking across to where Helen sat by a window above the courtyard.

At the end of the table opposite Priam, the Greek envoy, Palamedes, was standing, leaning forward a little and speaking eagerly.

'With Achilles out of the war, the Gweeks would have no chance,' he was saying. 'They'd make peace at once — certainly if you gave back Helen.'

'Never!' snapped Paris.

'Well, even without that,' continued Palamedes, shrugging his shoulders. 'Agamemnon's a coward. He's suggested wunning away two or thwee times alweady — only Odysseus and old Nestor always stop him. The old man has a lot of tall storwies about men being men when *he* was young; and that sly bwute Odysseus with one of his long arguments which no one can quite follow, but evwyone says is *so* wise. He's a bad lot — sly and a cheat. I wouldn't twust him an inch!'

'He'd trust you farther than that!' cried Helen, firing up. 'I've heard Odysseus say he'd trust you as far as he could kick you, but no farther!'

'A vulgar bwute,' said Palamedes. 'But what is this — this foreign woman doing here? Surely it's the Spartan vixen who started the whole war, isn't it?'

'You may insult your own countrymen as much as you like!' shouted Paris, springing up, with his sword half drawn. 'But if you don't keep your foul tongue from my wife, I'll tear it out first and then hang you head down from the highest tower of Troy for the vultures! And that's too good an end for a traitor like you!'

'Beg pardon!' murmured Palamedes. 'I thought it was King Menelaus's wife. But as I see there are even bigger bwutes in Twoy than there are in Gweece, I apologize to Pwince Parwis's bwide!'

'Is this the time for brawls and insults?' exclaimed Priam. 'Be silent, my son Paris. And for you, Lady Helen, as you may be sure that we shall never give you up, this council concerns you no farther. I give you leave to depart.'

Helen rose obediently, bowed slightly to the king, and walked quickly to the door. But as she reached it, she turned suddenly and said in clear, ringing tones, perfectly mimicking the voice of Menelaus, 'The King of Sparta knows how to avenge insults to his wife — whether made by a Greek or a Trojan!'

Then Helen was gone, but Palamedes sprang back, exclaiming shrilly, 'By Poseidon, that *was* the voice of Menelaus! What tweachewy are you Twojans plotting against me?'

'None, none!' exclaimed Paris impatiently. 'Helen has always had this gift of mimicry. She uses it to annoy me ... But let's get back to this chance of getting Achilles out of the war.'

'It's more than a chance, it's a definite offer,' said Palamedes, leaning forward over the table again, and speaking as impressively as he could. 'If you will give him your daughter to be his wife, give her fweely and by

her own will, Achilles pwomises and vows to fight no more against Twoy. If you give up Helen he will persuade the Gweeks to end the war altogether and go home. He may twy even without that: but he has fallen in love with your daughter, and is determined to have her. And Achilles always gets what he wants!'

Up in the roof-space Nico felt Polyxena start up suddenly and then crouch down again, trembling all over; and he vowed to himself that if *she* was the daughter meant, he'd do everything in his power to save her from being sacrificed, even to a Greek.

'It certainly is a good offer,' said Priam, and his two old councillors nodded their heads and murmured, 'Hear! Hear!', though Paris muttered angrily under his breath. 'Indeed a very good offer, as things are at the moment . . . I am prepared to accept it. But is this from Achilles alone, or does he speak for King Agamemnon, the commander of the Greeks?'

'No one knows about it except I myself,' replied Palamedes. 'I told Achilles I could get into Twoy and see you pwivately, King Pwiam. He didn't ask how, fortunately! I did the wounds of the sentinels this morning just before dawn – this way of posting sentinels was my own invention – and slipped into Twoy while those by the Skaian Gate were changing guard. So no one even knows I'm here. But you must decide quickly. Achilles has gone away to the island of Tenedos, but of course he can get back in a few hours. He's gone there to be purwified for killing Thersites who's a distant cousin of Odysseus. Thersites was a bwute. When Achilles killed your ally Penthesilia, Queen of the Amazons, he didn't know she was a woman until he began stwipping off her armour. Then he was sorwy, or pwetended to be, and even wept, like the silly fool he is. But Thersites laughed at him, and said he'd fall in love with any pwetty face, even a dead one; and he started jabbing the corpse with his spear. Then Achilles got into one of his terwible wages and stwuck Thersites on the side of the head with his fist so hard that he fwactured his skull and knocked all his teeth out — and Thersites died that verwy night. So Achilles had to be purwified for killing a Gweek of noble birth, and he and Odysseus set off. They said they were going to Lesbos, which would take a whole day to get to: but Achilles told me pwivately that he was going to Tenedos as soon as he'd got wid of Odysseus. Agamemnon won't go on with the war until Achilles comes back, and if he's away too long he'll send to look for him . . . I ought to go to Tenedos before this evening, in case Achilles gets tired of waiting and comes back. But I can't get out of Twoy until after dark.'

'Palamedes, I know that you wish me well,' said Priam solemnly. 'So I will trust you with a message to Achilles. He shall have Polyxena, but he must come here to woo her — and to swear the oath with his hand on the very Palladion which Zeus cast down from heaven to mark the site of Troy for Ilos my grandfather. Just as I came to his very hut in the midst of the Greeks to beg for the body of my dear son Hector, and came back in safety, so I vow that he shall come and return in safety.'

'Get him into Troy,' muttered Paris angrily. 'Get him in, and we'll see how safely he gets out again!'

'Paris!' Priam rose to his full height, and for a moment his age seemed to fall from him and once more he was the great king who had brought all Phrygia under his sway, and created out of the ruins left by Heracles when he was a boy a great city and a powerful alliance that all Greece feared.

'Paris, I sometimes doubt if you are indeed the son whom I once cast out to die upon Ida in obedience to the oracle. Have you no honour? No fear of the deathless gods? Oh, Cassandra was right: you will indeed bring shame and destruction upon Troy! But now, get you gone from my sight, and do not set foot inside the sacred precinct of the Temple of Pallas Athena again until I say the word – on pain of death! No, do not answer. Go!'

Paris had risen to his feet, his face flushed with anger. But the old king's voice and his power of command were too much for him. Without a word he turned and strode out of the room, and went clattering away down the steps and out into the Temple courtyard.

'Palamedes, son of Nauplius,' said Priam, still standing erect, 'I beg you to forgive the impious and unmannerly words of my son Paris. He was brought up among shepherds on Mount Ida – and he has always felt that our people blame him for bringing this war upon Troy: let these things excuse him. But once again, I repeat my solemn oath of safe conduct if you can bring Achilles into Troy . . . Antenor, show Palamedes the secret way so that he may bring Achilles to the Temple unseen and unknown to any except ourselves. But first take his oath upon the very Palladion that he will reveal the way to no one else at all save to Achilles alone. And arrange with him when Achilles is to come.'

'Farewell, gweat king,' said Palamedes, bowing low. 'I will tell Achilles all that has passed in this woom – not forgetting how you tweat impudent puppies like Pwince Parwis. And I am sure that he will come. To be in love is to be weady to take any wisk – and he has loved

Pwincess Polyxena from the moment that he saw her when she dwopped her bwacelet to wansom Hector.'

'Stay a moment, my cousin Antenor,' said Priam. 'As you pass the Treasury, give to Prince Palamedes as noble a gift as still remains to us of gold or jewels, that he may carry with him easily.'

Palamedes and Antenor went out of the room, and Nico could hear them in the Treasury underneath.

'Was it wise, my lord king, to tell this Greek the secret way into Troy?' asked old Anchises suddenly.

'It is certainly a risk,' answered Priam, pulling thoughtfully at his beard. 'But we must take risks now. At all costs we must keep Achilles out of the war – altogether, if possible; but certainly until our last ally, Memnon Prince of the Morning, comes to our aid . . . Moreover, my cousin, I trust this Palamedes . . . Well, he has not played us false yet.'

'But will you indeed give your daughter Polyxena to Achilles?' asked Anchises. 'To Achilles who has slain so many of her brothers? Hector, and Troilus, and Mestor and Lycaon, and –'

'Yes,' answered Priam, cutting short the catalogue firmly. 'It is right that one girl should be sacrificed to save Troy.'

At this Nico turned towards Polyxena – to find to his amazement that she was no longer there. Forgetting Priam and Anchises, he sprang to his feet and groped his way back to the wall separating him from the roof-space over the Temple.

It took him a little while to find the gap in the wall, and much longer to reach the small square hole in the corner and scramble through it and down the pegs in the beam on to the ledge in the shrine. There was still no sign of Polyxena, so he lowered himself carefully to the floor, and was about to steal out into the room where the lamp burnt dimly on the altar, when he heard footsteps approaching quickly.

There was no time to scramble back on to the ledge, so

Nico crouched down behind the big square pedestal of stone on which the Palladion stood. A moment later he heard the lamp lifted from the altar, saw the light flicker suddenly on the walls of the kella, and then — so suddenly that he almost sprang up and gave himself away — he heard Antenor say, 'Here, Prince Palamedes, rest your hand on this holy image, the very Palladion which came from heaven, and swear your oath — knowing that Pallas Athena knows your thoughts and hears your words, and would strike you dead if you broke it.'

'I swear, by Athena and her holy image,' said Palamedes, 'that I will tell or show to no one else except Achilles only whatever Antenor the Twojan shall show me.'

'Good,' said Antenor. 'Now watch what I do.'

The light of the lamp grew less, but Nico did not dare to look round the edge of the pedestal, for Antenor and Palamedes were still very near to him, or so it seemed.

Then he heard a sound of sliding metal, and a clash as of metal striking upon stone. After this he heard Palamedes breathing hard, and then exclaim aloud as if he had bumped or scraped himself.

A moment later Antenor said: 'Right. Now go straight ahead, only beware as you come out in the swamp . . . I will expect you at the time we agreed upon, unless I see the signal fire.'

Then there came a thud and a loud clang. A moment later footsteps sounded, walking slowly out of the Temple.

Cautiously Nico stole out from behind the pedestal of the Palladion. The lamp was back on the altar in the outer room; he could see Antenor walking away through the main doorway of the Temple. But Palamedes had gone.

Chapter 3

THE GREEK BEGGAR

When he had made sure that Palamedes was not hiding in the Temple, and that Antenor had left the sacred precinct, Nico set to work to discover the secret way out of Troy. But he could find nothing. Floor and walls seemed to be of solid stone, each block squared and fitted, and in most cases cemented in place. True, there was the drain behind the altar: but this consisted of a large slab of stone very slightly hollowed in the middle, in which were cut three long slits each a couple of inches wide.

Nico gave all his attention to the drain, but with no result. The slab appeared to be fixed as firmly as any of the other stones; the slits were far too narrow even for a man's foot to pass through, and from beneath came a slight sound of running water and an extremely unpleasant smell.

'It must be the over-flow from the basin in the upper courtyard on top of the citadel,' said Nico to himself. 'The water from the sacred spring that bubbles up there and runs along the marble channel into the tank. Yes, I remember now, it overflows from the basin, when the tank's full, and out through the carved lion's head in front and falls into the hole in the pavement below. But it's only a little drain, less than a foot square, and no one could possibly get through it . . . Anyhow, this drain-cover won't even shake . . . There must be a passage in the wall somewhere . . .'

But he looked in vain; and presently, hearing footsteps in the courtyard, he put back the lamp hastily on the square altar and looked cautiously out. It was Theano, Antenor's wife, the Priestess of Athena; but fortunately she went past the Temple in the direction of the Treasury.

Nico slipped out as soon as she had gone, ran across the courtyard and up the steps on to the wall by the gate of the precinct. Here a Temple guard challenged him, but gave a grunt when he saw who it was, and turned back to keep watch over the narrow street below which led to the gate. Nico ran on, along the wall, turned right at the corner, and on up the steps towards Helen's tower. As he went he saw Priam and Anchises walking slowly across the court-yard below, escorted by Antenor and Theano.

Nico passed another sentry, and ran up the last flight to the tower. He tapped at the door and entered quickly. Helen sat in her usual place by the window, gazing out over the plain where the Greek huts were clustered less than a quarter of a mile from the city, and away to the main camp far beyond and the ships drawn up on the seashore beyond that. Her eyes seemed large and dark with trouble, and the Star Stone trembled so that once again blood seemed to drip from it.

'What is it, mother?' asked Nico, quick suddenly to sense Helen's trouble.

'Paris!' Helen shuddered as she named him. 'Paris — that devil, that sorcerer! Nico, oh, Nico, you must be careful — keep out of sight — stay with me. Oh, if only Menelaus would come — come quickly! Oh, if something would happen quickly!'

'Mother, something *is* going to happen!' exclaimed Nico, and forthwith poured out his tale. 'But they shan't take Polyxena,' he ended. 'These barbarians shan't sell her to a foreigner – to Achilles!'

Helen sighed; but she smiled also. 'My poor Nico!' she said. 'Neither Greek nor Trojan, it seems! But don't worry about Polyxena. She has been with me, and – she loves Achilles just as he loves her. Both: in that moment at the ransoming of Hector . . . Oh, Aphrodite, lady of love, you have betrayed me, and betrayed Troy – do not betray these two!'

'Polyxena – Achilles!' Nico found his whole world toppling about him, and his brain seemed to spin. As Helen truly said, he did not know in his heart of hearts whether he was really a Greek or a Trojan.

But he was to learn, and that quickly. For, after more than nine years of creeping warfare, events began to move with a sudden rush towards the end.

It was on the very next day that the old Greek beggar came into Troy. Paris, who happened to be in command of the watch that night at the Skaian Gate, saw him in the early morning skulking in the bushes at the corner of the wall, and sent two men to catch him and bring him into Troy.

He was a shocking sight. Nico managed to slip down and see what was going on; for the Skaian Gate was immediately below Helen's tower, and Paris, who believed in comfort, carried out most of his duties as commander of the Skaian Gate reclining on a couch under the portico of a balcony above the Gate, about half-way up the side of the tower.

The Greek beggar was an oldish man with a ragged beard and a bad limp. He was dressed in filthy evil-smelling rags; and when these came away in the rough hands of the two guards who dragged him up the steep steps to the balcony, Nico saw that his back was all lined and criss-crossed with angry red weals edged here and there with the black crust of caked blood.

'Well?' asked Paris in a brisk, rather bored voice. 'What were you up to, prowling round Troy? Speak quickly, or I'll tell my men to drop you over the wall out of the way.'

'So please you, noble lord,' whined the beggar, speaking with a strong Argive accent, 'I've come to pray for shelter in Troy.'

'Oh, throw him over the wall!' exclaimed Paris wearily. 'We've enough mouths of our own to feed, without taking in beggars – who are probably Greek spies anyhow.'

'Spare me! Spare me, your excellency!' howled the beggar, tearing himself from the guards, and leaving even more of his filthy rags in their hands. 'I can help Troy to win the war! I know many secrets of the Greeks – and their new plan to capture Troy!'

He grovelled on the ground, and Paris, who had risen to his feet, kicked him impatiently.

'Speak quickly,' he snapped. 'Who and what are you, and how can you help us?'

'I'm a Greek, I admit it,' answered the beggar, sitting up slowly. 'My name is Irus, and I was a charioteer from Mycenae. King Agamemnon lent me to his cousin King Penelaus of Boeotia, but I was wounded with a spear by noble Hector. Look, it tore my leg and severed all the tendons, so that I can only limp, and am no use as a fighting man.' He pointed to a long white scar on the inside of his leg above his left knee; then he went on: 'That was many years ago, when first we landed down over there by the sea. I was a strong and skilful charioteer then, and not meanly born. In Mycenae I stood on guard in the very palace of Agamemnon: yes, I was personal guard to the princesses his daughters and to the Princess Hermione of Sparta when she came to live in Mycenae after Helen had fled with you, noble Prince of Troy. But when I was no longer of use as a charioteer, King Agamemnon commanded me to serve that most evil of men, Odysseus of Ithaca. I was to be a guard outside his hut, since I could no longer stand in a chariot or march to battle. But he made me a mere slave. When I became ill with fever, he threw me out to die. But I didn't die; only I was too weak to work, and could only live by begging. I became useful to the Greek princes, however, and did errands for them in spite of my lameness. But when Achilles murdered Thersites, who was a kind friend to me, I demanded his punishment in the full Assembly – as even a common soldier has a right to do. But I was a fool: they could not forgive me for that. The Greeks would do anything to please Achilles and keep him here at Troy – for they know that without him you would defeat them easily. If Achilles hadn't come back to the war when Patroclus was killed, you'd have burnt the ships and destroyed the camp – and killed us all, or made slaves of us. Well, they couldn't do anything about me in the Assembly – and Achilles had to set off to Lesbos to be purified for the murder of Thersites. Odysseus went with him. But before he went he thrashed me, and locked me up in one of his huts. I stayed there without food or drink for three days. But yesterday Diomedes, who is the special friend of that monster from Ithaca, dragged me out, flogged me with a hide whip as you see, and then had me kicked out of the camp after giving orders that I should be stabbed or shot on sight if I should try to enter it again. I hid in the marsh, and this morning I crept up to the gate of Troy, determined to seek your help, and throw in my lot with you Trojans.'

'My good fellow,' exclaimed Paris, getting in a word at last as Irus the beggar paused for breath, 'you don't really think that all this rigmarole interests me, do you?'

'Of course not, Prince Paris,' hastened Irus, 'but I tell you so that you may know who I am and why I have such good cause to hate my own people the Greeks . . . What you want to know is, naturally, only what will be of use to you. I can tell you of many things – from the date of Achilles's return, to the plans which Odysseus is making for the capture of Troy.'

'All right,' said Paris. 'I'll tell the King about you, and later in the day I expect he'll call a council and question you. But be careful that you speak the truth: there are slower ways of dying than a fall from the wall over there: slower ways than you Greeks know about, and less – pleasant. The Phrygians are experts, and I've – studied the art.'

Then, turning to the guard, he added, 'All right. Take him to the guard-house. Feed him, and keep him safely until he's sent for.'

All morning Nico wandered disconsolately about Troy. He could not find Polyxena, and hardly knew whether he wanted to, or what he could say to her when he did. But he did want to hear what Irus the Greek beggar told Priam and the Trojan Council, and he kept a watch on the guard-house by the Skaian Gate. When Irus was led out, however, Paris was still in charge of the guard, and when Nico came down from the edge of the Temple precinct to follow into Priam's palace, he turned on him angrily.

'Get out, you Greek cub!' he shouted. 'If I find you

spying into matters which don't concern you, I'll break a few of your bones to keep you quiet. I'd have broken your neck long ago, if I'd had my way.'

Nico drew back hastily, but not so quickly that Irus the Greek beggar had not a moment to shoot him a glance out of grey eyes grown suddenly clear and penetrating. Then he screwed them up again, and went limping on after Paris: but Nico felt as if that glance had looked into his very heart, and read and recorded all there was to know about him.

After the palace doors had closed behind Paris and his captive, Nico went slowly up the stairs to Helen's tower and told her all that he had seen and heard.

Helen was troubled. 'I don't like it at all,' she said. 'It seems as if Achilles is going to make peace on his own and retire from the War; and then I don't think the Greeks will have much chance. If this beggar is a traitor and gives away the secret councils of Agamemnon and the other princes, there'll be even less chance . . . And if he's really a spy for the Greeks, it means they're getting desperate. I wonder if they know why Achilles is trying to leave – and about Palamedes coming here as his private envoy . . . I wish I could have a word with this beggar . . . But I don't want to ask Paris for *any* favour.'

Helen's wish was, however, granted unexpectedly. Late in the afternoon there came a tramp of feet on the stairs, the door was flung open and in strode Paris.

'Helen,' he said abruptly, 'I've brought you a countryman of yours. It's a filthy old beggar called Irus, who sought shelter in Troy, after being driven out by that cruel devil Odysseus and that brute Diomedes. He's given us such useful information that the King commands you to entertain him kindly – see that he's washed and given

74

decent clothes and so on . . . And of course we expect you to use all your arts to get even more useful information from him . . . All right, bring him in.'

Two guards led Irus into the room, saluted, and marched out.

'Now then,' said Paris sharply, 'this is my wife, the Princess Helen of Troy. As you're her countryman, she will entertain you. But mind you behave yourself, or it will be the worse for you . . . There's a guard on the wall outside, Helen, if you need one. I'd let your women attend to his old baggage: he's not fit for personal attention from a princess.'

When Paris had gone, Helen turned to Irus, who bowed low before her, with his eyes cast down.

'Tell me of my dear lord Menelaus!' she cried eagerly. 'Tell me news of my daughter Hermione, and of the lovely land of Greece, my home that I long to see again.'

'The King of Sparta still lives,' answered Irus, 'and what wounds he has received have all healed well. As for our lovely homeland, lady, I saw it for the last time only a little later than you did. For when you fled from Sparta with Paris less than a year passed before the fleet set sail from Aulis. I saw your daughter, the little princess Hermione, when I visited Mycenae not long before the fleet sailed, and I heard it said that she was in great sorrow and blamed her mother by whose flight she had lost not only mother and brother, but father too – since we all guessed that the war would be long.'

Then Helen put her face in her hands and wept for a little while.

'My countryman,' she said at last, looking up with dim eyes at the beggar, 'I swear to you before Zeus – and so I would that you could tell my dear lord Menelaus – that I did not run away with hateful Paris by my own will. And, oh, how I have longed through all these years to be at home again — to see the snow on Taygetos above the dear Eurotas stream, or golden Mycenae growing out of its mighty walls above the green and silver land of Argos. Yes, or even Athens, Athena's city, with its temples and its citadel on the sharp rock which I saw once when I was a girl and Theseus carried me away to Aphidna . . . Oh, I would rather be a shepherdess on Mount Cithaeron — if I had but the husband and the daughter whom I love — than queen of all Troy, yes of all Phrygia . . . But come now and let me see to your comfort. You must be washed, and those horrible cuts on your back need attention. Then I'll find you some decent clothes, and we will sit and eat together and talk of our home. And Nicostratus here shall listen: for though Greece is his home too, he has no real remembrance of it.'

When the beggar had been bathed and anointed by Helen's slave-girls, his hair and beard trimmed and oiled, and he had been dressed in a simple Phrygian tunic and mantle, Nico thought that he looked like a noble warrior or even a king.

Helen thought so too, for after gazing at him intently for a while, she said in a low voice, 'My lord Odysseus, you play a stranger part than ever we thought in those old days when you came to Sparta as my suitor.'

'Lady Helen!' The beggar sat back with his mouth open and his eyes wide with surprise. 'Surely you are joking? You cannot be trying to insult me? I've told you how much I hate Odysseus, and with what good cause. Even to suggest that I am like him is unkind of you.'

'Forgive me, good Irus,' said Helen, with a wan smile. 'But you are like Odysseus, or like Odysseus as I remember him, but grown older with suffering as well as time – as Odysseus must be by now . . . How I wish you were really Odysseus, with news that my long nightmare is at last drawing to an end!'

'Lady,' answered Irus, 'to please you I could pretend to be the man you name. But what use would that be? And what use is it to speak of even your first husband, Menelaus, since I am here to plot his downfall and the destruction of all the Greek leaders – particularly Odysseus?'

'Ah well,' said Helen, 'who is to suffer from your coming into Troy is for the gods to decide – for they alone know the truth concerning both you and me. But now, before we eat, let me do honour, through you, to all those in Greece whom I love – and to all those who war against Troy for my unworthy sake.'

So saying, she took up a bowl of warm water, set it on the ground beside Irus, and knelt down to wash his feet.

'No, no, lady Helen,' he exclaimed anxiously, 'I am no more than a poor beggar, and you are Queen of Sparta – or Princess of Troy!'

'If the former,' answered Helen quietly, 'all the more need that I do penance for the ills which I have brought upon Sparta and all Greece by my beauty . . . If the latter – I have a feeling that greater queens of Troy than I shall ever claim to be will be washing Greek feet before long.'

As she spoke, she drew back the tunic from the beggar's knees and bathed the long white scar that ran upwards on the inside of his left thigh. 'Which Trojan slave woman will you choose?' she continued, a ring of triumph in her voice. 'Shall it be Hecuba the queen, or her daughter, the prophetess Cassandra – or Paris's bride-by-capture, luckless Helen of Troy, who shall wash the feet of

Odysseus of Ithaca — yes, and this scar which the boar made when as a boy you hunted on Mount Parnassus with your grandfather Autolycus!'

There was a long silence; and then the beggar said quietly, 'Helen, I cannot pretend any longer. I am, as you say, none other than Odysseus — who was your friend and the friend of your husband Menelaus in those long ago, happy days when we came to Sparta — when we followed you and found you and brought you safely home to marry Menelaus, after Theseus had stolen you as you prayed in the temple of Artemis in the marsh by the Eurotas river . . . And now that you have discovered my secret, what do you propose to do? Give me up to Paris?'

'Give you up? Oh!' Helen clasped Odysseus by the knees and wept; and after a moment he leant forward and comforted her.

'That was unkind of me,' he said. 'But I am in such great danger, and — how could I be sure, now, whether your first loyalty was to Greece or to Troy?'

'To Greece, always to Greece,' sobbed Helen. 'To my dear, dear Menelaus, and you, my best friend. To the land which the gods love and have made the most beautiful upon earth, and have given to men worthy of it — not to this evil city of barbarians who do not even know the meaning of honour. Barbarians whose prince comes with the sacred name of guest, and steals away his host's wife and child, and robs his palace — and would murder ambassadors. Now tell me why you are here. Is it to save me and Nicostratus and restore us to Menelaus? Nico, come here! This is Odysseus, your father's dearest friend, of whom I have so often told you.'

All this while Nico had been sitting in the shadow near the window watching all that happened and listening to what was said. If his mind had been confused before, it was in a positive whirl now . . . Odysseus! In Troy! To Nico 'Odysseus' meant two different people: the wonderful hero and friend of whom his mother had told him so often, and the dreadfully cruel and wicked ogre with whom he and the children of Troy had been frightened for almost as long as he could remember.

And now here was the man himself – not the fiend in bronze armour whom he had seen in the distance on the plain of Troy, nor the fairytale prince shining in his imagination as, he felt sure, the gods themselves must shine – but a real person, looking at him with kindly grey eyes and resting a hand on his shoulder.

'Nicostratus. Yes. He's like his father. Menelaus has often spoken of his son – the child who was lost when Helen was taken . . . And Hermione, I remember, cried for her baby brother as well as for her mother. Menelaus and I went straight to Mycenae when we returned from Troy – after Antenor saved us from being murdered on Paris's orders, ambassadors though we were. Hermione was living at Mycenae with her cousins. But Clytemnestra has sent her back to Sparta, I hear. For Iphigeneia is dead, and Mycenae is not the happy home it was.' Odysseus sighed. 'I fear that few of our homes are as we left them. After ten years many of us may find troubles waiting for us . . . Now, Nicostratus, son of Menelaus, you can help us: for you are one of us, and you live actually in Troy, and know it better than I can, however long I remain here in disguise.'

'One of us.' The quiet way in which Odysseus said this, and the certainty in his voice as if stating an obvious fact, seemed to send an ice-cold splash of water over Nico. He woke on that instant from any Trojan dreams

that may have haunted him and striven to master him. He was a Greek: he was the son of Menelaus, King of Sparta: this man Odysseus was his countryman; all those hosts beleaguering Troy were his countrymen come to rescue him and Helen, and punish Paris and the barbarians of Troy.

'Yes, Odysseus of Ithaca,' he said. 'I can and will help in any way possible against those of our enemies in Troy . . . But – but –' and his voice shook suddenly. 'They are not all equally bad. Please try to save Polyxena. And there's Antenor and Theano too . . . I know I should hate all Trojans – but Polyxena has been my friend, and Antenor and his wife have helped and protected me – us, so often.'

'I understand.' Odysseus smiled kindly, and the hard glint went out of his eyes. 'And of course all Trojans are not evil. Some might almost be taken for Greeks. There was Hector, now: a very noble foeman, fighting in a bad cause: if only his word had swayed Priam this war might never have come about – or not yet, not with your mother as the pretext. And Aeneas too is an honourable man: I wish he had thrown in his cause with us – and Antenor too. Yes, your father and I owe our lives to Antenor. Tell him that when we enter Troy he has but to hang a leopard skin from the upper window of his house, and no Greek shall enter it or hurt any who take shelter with him or his family or servants. But Troy has not yet fallen . . . Helen, are we safe here from discovery? Can anyone come on us unawares, or will anyone overhear us?'

'When my two slave-girls have brought the food and wine – they're now down below, well out of ear-shot – I'll send them away,' answered Helen. 'That will leave only old Aethra in the little room half-way down the inner stairs – and she, poor dear, has been childish almost since we came to Troy.'

'Aethra, the mother of Theseus?' exclaimed Odysseus. 'So she is still alive! Her two grandsons Demophon and Acamas are with us to bring her home, or take her bones for honourable burial at Athens. They learnt that she was with you in Troy, and only joined Agamemnon's fleet for that reason, as of course they were not among your suitors who swore to rescue you if anyone carried you off.'

'You remember at Aphidna that she insisted on becoming my slave, to make up for the great wrong her son Theseus tried to do me,' said Helen. 'When Paris carried us off she followed to rescue me – or raise the alarm. Paris caught her, and would have killed her: but I suppose he decided that I ought to have one female attendant, and so he brought her too. He does not know who she is – I thought it safer for her sake. And when her mind gave way, it was easy.'

'She must be over ninety by now, surely?' murmured Odysseus. 'But, Helen, we have more important matters to discuss. Some food and wine first would, however, be a great help.'

Helen summoned the two slave-girls, and they drew up a polished table with metal feet. On it they placed besides cold meat, a great bowl, and by it an onion on a bronze plate, a measure of barley-meal, honey and goats'-milk cheese. Then, when she had sent the girls away, Helen mixed the honey and the barley in the bowl, with slices of onion to add relish, and grated the cheese over it with a bronze grater, and mixed all this with the dark fiery wine made on Mount Pramne in the island of Icaria, far away to the south of Troy.

'We have no golden cups left in Troy,' she said in apology as she poured out the drink into a two-handed goblet, also of bronze. 'It has all gone to pay the allies — or buy fresh ones.'

Odysseus applied himself to the small portion of cold meat without answering. But when this was finished he raised the cup, poured a few drops on to the floor in reverence to Athena, and then drank to Helen.

'I feel better now!' he exclaimed. 'Ready for whatever may come! The meat was somewhat scanty, but the wine was good.'

'There is little meat in Troy these days,' answered Helen, and Odysseus nodded shrewdly.

'Our siege is drawing tighter and tighter,' he said. 'If only Agamemnon had listened to me, we'd have starved Troy out long ago. But, of course, while Hector lived there could be no real siege . . . Priam has another ally, the last, I believe: Memnon. He may break through if he comes before Achilles returns from Lesbos, but not for long.'

'Is Achilles really in Lesbos?' asked Nico suddenly. 'Palamedes told Priam that he was only in Tenedos — he could be back at Troy in two or three hours.'

'Palamedes!' Odysseus set down his cup with a clatter and stared at Nico. 'When? How? Has *he* been into Troy? Tell me quickly!'

So Nico told all that he and Polyxena had overheard in the room behind the Temple of Pallas Athena, and Helen added when he had finished, 'I too have seen Palamedes in Troy, and certainly Achilles seems anxious to win Polyxena. As she fell in love with him the moment she saw him, it seems likely that if he and Priam can meet they'll make some agreement which will keep Achilles out of the war. And if Memnon comes after that, both Priam and Paris believe that Troy may still win.'

'The danger is real,' said Odysseus, 'for Memnon is near even now. We are ready for him – even if Achilles does not come in time, or avoids fighting. But it's this business of Palamedes that interests me. I've always disliked that lisping jackass with his superior airs: but perhaps it's a personal hatred – he did me a bad turn once – and even jealousy. He's nearly as famed for his cunning as I am; and his inventions are certainly beyond me. His latest is a game called "dice", which kept the men amused all through last winter when there might well have been a mutiny. But nevertheless I'd like to know whether any double-dealing's going on here. Is he doing this out of friendship for Achilles – or to help Priam? I wonder . . . Is he a spy for us of Greece, or a traitor?'

'You've come here as a spy yourself,' Helen reminded him, with a smile. 'Or had you some secret message for anyone in Troy – like Palamedes?'

Odysseus laughed. 'I deserved that,' he said, 'though I'm serious, and I think unbiased, in my doubts about Palamedes. I had, perhaps, a message for you: Menelaus begged me while I was in Troy to find out how – well, how you were and what your feelings were as to the outcome of the war. Also I was to find out about Nicostratus. But I had a real reason for coming, besides that of simply spying. It's all the doing of Calchas the seer: it seems to me that even if Agamemnon commands the Allied Achaians, Calchas commands Agamemnon – and the common soldiers.'

Odysseus paused and shivered. 'It was Calchas who prophesied that the Greek fleet could not leave Aulis unless a king's maiden daughter was sacrificed by her own free will,' he said. 'And he has added that just such another sacrifice must be performed before we can leave Troy after the city has been destroyed . . . Oh yes, he's certain that Troy will fall, and in this, the tenth year: we all saw the sign of it sent from Zeus. But now he says that, in spite of the sign, Troy cannot fall while the Palladion remains in it. And the soldiers all believe him. They'll mutiny if an attack is ordered without the Palladion, though of course they'll fight outside on the plain if Memnon comes, or if any Trojans dare to leave the city. But they will not so much as cast a stone at any gate of Troy until they see the Palladion, the Luck of Troy, outside the walls. I've learnt from Trojan prisoners that the Palladion is an image of Pallas which fell from heaven to mark the site of Troy when King Laomedon built the earlier city. I gather it's the most sacred object in all Troy, and I've volunteered to come and get it, together with what information I can. No one else dared, or could think of any scheme — certainly not Palamedes, which makes me even more suspicious now that you tell me he knows a secret way in and out of Troy. But tell me, how big is this Palladion? Where is it? And can you help me to carry it off?'

'The Palladion is in the Temple of Athena, just below here,' said Helen. 'And it's quite small. I've seen Theano the High Prietess bring it out and hold it up before the people at festivals, or in times of special trouble. Yes, it would fit into that leather beggar's bag of yours.'

'And now, in the heat of the day, no one is likely to be near the Temple,' exclaimed Nico, eager and frightened at the same moment.

'Then, as there's no time like the present, let's go down at once,' said Odysseus. 'After all, why shouldn't you take the poor beggar Irus to pray in Athena's Temple, now that he's left the cruel Greeks and thrown in his lot for good or ill with the noble Trojans?'

So Helen led the way down the stairs, past the little room where old Aethra sat embroidering with invisible threads in a frame that was not there a great tapestry of the many deeds of her long-dead son Theseus. Out on to the wall they went, and down the steps into the empty courtyard, even the two guards being apparently asleep or sheltering elsewhere from the glaring noon-tide sun.

Down in the courtyard the heat was almost unbearable, striking up off the stone pavement and out from the walls on every side. It was like walking into an oven.

'Nico's right,' whispered Odysseus, who as the beggar Irus was now limping abjectly behind Helen. 'No one in their sense would come here at this time of day – not if they wanted to keep their senses.'

Helen led the way up the Temple steps and into the shadow of the pillars. The sun was less glaring there, but the heat even more stifling, and Helen went quickly into the Temple, followed by the limping Odysseus, Nico bringing up the rear with a beating heart – afraid and exultant. Afraid with the scrap of Trojan that still seemed to lurk in him, and exultant as a Greek, and the son of a great Greek king, striking his first blow for his father and his father's people.

'Here we are,' said Helen in a low voice. 'And in there behind the altar stands the Palladion itself – oh!'

Helen screamed suddenly as a figure stepped out from behind the altar, and she saw that it was none other than Queen Hecuba, while behind her the lamplight flashed on a drawn sword held by somebody inside the shrine itself.

Chapter 4

ACHILLES IN TROY

'Helen!' Hecuba drew herself up and her eyes seemed to flash in the lamplight. 'What are you doing here? And with this man who is, I understand, a Greek renegade who has sought shelter among us – and may well be a spy in disguise!'

'Paris told me to look after him –' began Helen, completely unnerved for the moment.

'And you begin by bringing him to the Temple of Pallas,' said Hecuba grimly, 'to the most sacred place in Troy, where the very Palladion stands. Helen, I have always tried to befriend and help you – I have treated you as my son Paris's wife. But I expect you to be loyal to Paris, and to Troy, and not to betray us to the Greeks, even if they are your own people. And now I find you bringing this man into the Temple at a time when you must have felt certain that it would be empty . . . I suppose I must not blame you, but this man surely deserves to die. We cannot let him get out of Troy and tell the Greeks our most hidden secrets. Stand aside, Helen, and my guards here shall cut him down – or shoot him with their arrows if he attempts to run away.'

Nico made a move forward as if to come between Odysseus and the entrance of the shrine. But Odysseus motioned him back with a quick jerk of the hand and stepped forward, all trace of his limp gone.

'Queen Hecuba,' he said in his own quiet, strong voice,

87

'I am your suppliant.' With a quick movement he knelt before her, touching her knees with one hand and raising the other to her face. 'Listen a moment. You are both right and wrong. I am not the beggar Irus whom I pretended to be – in fact I am Odysseus, King of Ithaca . . . Hear me still further. I have not come, as you might think, as a mere spy. No, I come on behalf of great Achilles himself. I am in his secrets, and I know of his love for your daughter Polyxena and that he has offered, if you will give her to him in marriage, to retire from the war, and do his best to persuade Agamemnon to make peace and return home with all his army.'

'Odysseus, Troy's worst enemy,' said Hecuba slowly. 'Why has Achilles sent you to us like this? We have already received his messenger and delivered our answer – and told him how he may enter Troy unobserved and in safety to speak with Polyxena and swear to us on the very Palladion that he will no longer fight against his wife's people . . . Odysseus, you who are known as the "master of many wiles", I do not believe you.'

'Alas that you should be so deceived!' exclaimed Odysseus. 'The messenger who came to you from Achilles was Palamedes, was it not? Well, he is a man whom nobody can trust – and even Achilles felt that he must have an independent witness before he ventured into Troy. So I came, disguised as a beggar. Even the lady Helen did not know who I really was. But I told her why I had come, and she was bringing me down now to swear with my hand on the Palladion that what I said was true . . . Now, Queen of Troy, if I have but your word, I can go back to Achilles fully assured that all will be well with him – and with Troy. So tell me that in this case Palamedes spoke the truth, and then send me straight out of

Troy to bear your assurance to Achilles . . . You must make haste, for our scouts tell us that your husband's nephew Memnon and his followers are near at hand, and if they reach Troy before Achilles has sworn his oath to you, he will fight against them – and even the Prince of the Morning has no chance against Achilles.'

There was a long pause, and Nico held his breath until he could hear his own heart beating loudly in the silence.

Then Hecuba said, 'Odysseus, though I have no cause to wish you well, this time I will spare your life. But go quickly from Troy, and do not attempt to enter the city again. Listen: I swear to you that Achilles may come with safety into Troy, and go safely out again by the way which Palamedes knows and will show him.'

'I thank you, noble Queen,' said Odysseus, kissing Hecuba's feet, as a suppliant should whose prayer has been granted. 'Now I'll go as swiftly as I can to Achilles. Can I perhaps leave Troy by this secret gate of which you speak?'

Hecuba paused for a moment, but then said, 'No, I must not reveal it to you; even Helen does not know. But she doubtless can help you to escape. Helen, take this man away from the Temple, and do not let me see him again, for if I do I shall tell Paris who he is. And if Paris knows that it is Odysseus, he will not let him leave Troy alive.'

Helen turned without a word and walked slowly out of the Temple, Odysseus following her, once more the limping shifty-eyed beggar Irus.

Nico, who all this time had been standing back in the shadow near the entrance of the Temple, stepped forward slowly to follow them. As he did so he heard Antenor's voice from inside the shrine say in an undertone, 'Send him to fetch your sister and Polyxena. Palamedes should be here at any moment, and I'd rather not leave you alone in the Temple.'

'Nicostratus,' called Hecuba, and she smiled kindly as the boy turned back and looked at her anxiously. 'Nico, dear, there's nothing to worry about. But you mustn't let your mother meddle in affairs like this, or I don't know what Paris may do – and I've very little control over him, I'm afraid, certainly where Helen's concerned. It's all right: she didn't know it was Odysseus, and he'll be safe enough so long as none of my sons discover who he is – particularly Paris and Deiphobus. But I want you to do something for me. Will you run round to the room over the Treasury where you'll find the Priestess Theano and Polyxena. Tell them to come into the Temple immediately: Theano will know why. Then you'd better go straight up to Helen's tower to be out of the way. Run now, child!'

Nico bowed obediently to the Queen, and ran quickly out of the temple and round between the wall and the pillars where he was still shaded from the burning sun.

'It's a good thing the Queen forgets how old I am!' he thought as he went. 'She thinks I'm still too young to understand anything about what's happening ... But what is happening? I wish I knew! I *must* know!'

Nico ran up the steps outside the Treasury, tapped at the door and went in quickly. Theano, the old priestess, was sitting at her embroidery frame at one side of the room, while Polyxena knelt by the window, looking out across the courtyard to the walls and buildings which separated it from Helen's tower. She sprang up eagerly as the door opened, but looked disappointed when she saw that it was Nico.

'Hello!' she exclaimed. 'What are you doing here?'

'Queen Hecuba sent me with a message,' said Nico. 'She wants both you and your aunt in the Temple at once. Antenor is there too.'

'All right, dear, we'll come in a moment,' said Theano, getting up slowly from her chair. 'Polyxena, my child, what are you thinking of? Put on your veil at once: you know who it is we are going to meet!'

Polyxena blushed furiously, and snatched up the silk veil which most of the younger women in Troy still used, after the eastern fashion.

Nico looked on in surprise, for until a few weeks ago he and Polyxena had wandered where they liked in Troy, alone and as scantily clad as they cared to be. Yes, definitely Helen was right: Polyxena had grown up suddenly, and Nico had lost his playmate. For a desperate moment something seemed to rise up inside him and shout that it wasn't true, he mustn't let it be true; and in his unreasoning panic to escape from this new life into which it seemed that he was being forced suddenly, he exclaimed, as he might have done a month ago, 'Come on, Poly, I'll race you to the Temple!'

Polyxena flushed and seemed about to answer angrily; but a new thought swept over her and the anger turned to exaltation in her eyes.

'No, Nico,' she said quietly. 'Those days are over. I am the Princess of Troy going to meet the Prince of the Myrmidons, and I go as a princess should.'

So saying she put the veil over her head and swept out of the room with a dignity that rivalled Hecuba's own, while Nico fell back in confusion.

'Dear, dear, these girls do grow up so quickly!' exclaimed Theano fussily as she hurried after Polyxena.

91

'Now then, Nico, you shut up here after me, there's a good boy. You know where the key goes.'

Theano bustled down the steps and round the corner of the Temple to catch up with Polyxena, and Nico found himself alone in the doorway with the T-shaped bronze key in his hand.

But now his mind was made up: 'If Polyxena's the Princess of Troy,' he said under his breath, 'I'm the Prince of Sparta. I must find out what those Trojans are doing in the Temple with Palamedes the traitor, and see whether Achilles is really there . . . I must also find where this secret entrance is.'

Nico went back into the room, shutting the door after him and pushing the bolt across. Two pegs in a beam at one corner told him that the entrance to the roof-space must be there; and sure enough as he scrambled up a loose square of wood in the corner of the ceiling rose easily as his head touched it. A few moments later he was stepping cautiously from beam to beam until he came to the gap in the wall at the back of the shrine of the Palladion through which he and Polyxena had crawled when they came from the other side to spy on Palamedes's conference with Priam.

As he reached the wall Nico could hear voices from beyond it, and looking cautiously through the square opening in the corner he saw that a lamp was burning in the shrine lighting up the dark room with a rather lurid, smoky light. Standing in front of the Palladion was a group consisting of Hecuba, Antenor, Theano, Polyxena, Palamedes – and Achilles.

'Queen of Troy,' Achilles was saying in the strong, sharp voice of one always accustomed to give orders – and to have his own way – 'you are in too great a hurry. I've come, under pledge of safety, merely to speak with the Princess Polyxena alone. So now leave us together here. Palamedes, you can wait outside the Temple, and keep watch in case of any danger. Take the Princess's attendant with you . . . I beg pardon, the priestess Theano.'

'My lord Achilles,' said Hecuba with great dignity, 'I will do as you wish. But you must understand that you come here in safety only because it is Polyxena's wish, and in the hope that you and she may find a way of ending this dreadful war . . . It is for the sake of Troy, otherwise you surely cannot think that I could agree to any alliance with the man who killed Hector and Troilus, to say nothing of the many other leaders of the Trojans and our allies.'

Achilles laughed lightly. 'You cannot fight a war without killing men,' he said. 'Naturally I did my best to destroy as many of your leaders as possible . . . You may now add your husband's nephew, Memnon, whom I met in battle last night on his way to Troy – before which he will not now appear, unless I drag him at my chariot wheels.'

This silenced Hecuba, who seemed quite overcome by the news, and Antenor led her quickly out of the Temple. Palamedes then turned to Theano.

'Come along, old lady!' he cried. 'We're wather in the way, don't you think? Let's leave these two love-birds in here and go outside for a bit. No? Well, you can wait just inside the Temple out of the sun, and we'll hope you're nice and deaf. I'm going out to stwetch my legs under the portico. A bit of air, however hot, will be nice after that nasty, smelly secwet passage of yours.'

As soon as Palamedes and Theano had gone Achilles turned to Polyxena and took a quick step in her direction. But she held up her hands as if to push him away, and said very quietly, 'My lord Achilles, before we speak of — of matters which concern ourselves, you must promise me, with your hand here on the very Palladion that if — if I answer as you wish, you will make peace with my father and do your best to end this war.'

Achilles laughed again in his easy fashion. 'Indeed, dear heart!' he cried, 'I hoped that you would take me for myself, and not as a ransom for Troy. But as you helped to ransom your dead brother — well, ransoming seems to be rather a Trojan habit. So be easy, my pretty Trojan. I'm tired of Agamemnon and his tantrums, and Menelaus who couldn't look after his wife when he had her, and has been moaning after her ever since, and that wise Odysseus who'll get into trouble one day if he doesn't stop being so clever, yes and that dear, stupid Ajax — and certainly of that old bore Nestor, who would talk the tail off a mermaid and then explain how they grew new ones when he was young. Yes, Agamemnon's so swelled-headed that I've already had one quarrel with him, as I'm sure you know: if my poor cousin Patroclus hadn't gone out in my armour to frighten Paris the coward and the rest of you Trojans, he and his friends would have been your prisoners by now. But never mind that, I'm ready for another quarrel with him. So you and I'll go sailing over the sea to Greece, leaving him to run away when next he feels like it — and when Odysseus isn't waiting to catch him by the collar and bring him back. Oh, I've had a fine war, and won deathless fame, killing Hector and Memnon and the rest of them. But it was foretold that I would die in this war, and that I must choose between great fame or long life. I chose fame, of course — and having won that, I'd like to prove these seers wrong. Particularly that nasty piece of work,

Agamemnon's prophet Calchas, who I'm sure would like to sacrifice you if he could.

'But that's enough about such dull subjects. There now, with my hand on your Palladion, I swear that if you'll be mine, I'll make peace with your father and sail home to Greece as soon as you'll come with me . . . And now I swear with my hand on yours, sweet Polyxena, that I love you, and have loved you from the first moment that I saw you . . .'

Nico rose rather quickly, tiptoed back through the roof space and let himself down into the room above the Treasury. Opening the door, he went out, closed it behind him, and inserting the end of the key through the hole he pushed the wooden bolt into place, tied the cord which could be used to draw it, and slipped the key into a cranny in the wall.

Then he went cautiously down the steps and stood for a few moments in the shadow of the pillars, wondering what to do.

But he was not left in doubt for long. Suddenly Palamedes came in sight round the corner of the Temple, looked carefully to see that no one was about, and then walked swiftly across the courtyard and up the narrow steps towards the pathway along the wall that led both to the look-out over the Skaian Gate and to Helen's tower.

'That's something I can do — keep an eye on Palamedes,' thought Nico as he remembered what Odysseus had said about the doubtful character of the Prince of Nauplia.

'Achilles told him to stay on guard outside the Temple, so what's he doing up there? Of course, Achilles may have told him to do something else after I went . . . Or

perhaps he's looking for Priam or Hecuba to tell them that Achilles is ready to discuss the peace terms.'

Palamedes seemed to know his way about, for when he reached the guard-point just out of sight of the courtyard, Nico heard him give the pass-word as the guard challenged him. Then he saw him hurrying along the wall towards the cool watch-room below Helen's tower where Paris was usually to be found.

As soon as he was out of sight, Nico dashed across the courtyard and up the long flight of narrow steps to the top of the wall. As he swung round the corner, the guard who was lolling back in the shade clashed forward to attention, but relapsed with a grunt of disgust when he saw who it was.

'Only children and madmen run about at this time o' day!' he growled. 'Can't a poor chap have forty winks when all the rest o' the sensible world's having its midday sleep? Oh, er – if you're goin' up to the tower an' your stepfather's there, you might tell 'im he's wanted urgently in the watch-room. News about this Prince Memnon who's coming to fight for us. That's what the man said. Funny chap, talks like a Greek and looks like a Phoenician, but has the pass-word as pat as a Trojan.'

'I'll tell Paris,' said Nico, 'so you'd better keep awake until he comes down! Only Phrygians and fleas sleep standing up!'

'Greek gutter-snipe!' shouted the guard, hitting out with his clenched fist. But Nico dodged deftly so that he barked his knuckles on the stone wall, and he left him swearing savagely as he dashed on up the steps.

At the top Nico stopped, and walked quietly into Helen's tower and tiptoed up the steps past Aethra's little room until he reached Helen's door. There was no sound, so he went in quickly, and found her sitting alone by the window, gazing out as usual towards the Greek camp and the blue line of the sea beyond the brown plain.

'Mother!' exclaimed Nico breathlessly, 'is all safe here?'

'Yes, my dear,' answered Helen, coming out of a dream with an effort. 'There's only Aethra in the tower. Odysseus went some time ago: he'd a plan of his own for getting out of Troy. All he wanted to know was where the guard-rooms were, I suppose so as to keep away from them. But you look excited: has anything happened?'

'I should think it has!' Nico poured out his tale with a rush. 'Achilles is down in the Temple with Polyxena, and she's going to marry him, and he'll make peace with Priam and sail away with her to Greece, and he's killed Memnon, and Palamedes is with him, only he isn't any more. He's looking for Paris, and I don't think he's up to any good, but whether he's betraying us or the Trojans I don't know.'

Helen rose to her feet and walked up and down the room anxiously.

'He *must* be a traitor,' she said. 'He wouldn't risk getting mixed up with Paris otherwise. Paris hits first and thinks afterwards — if he ever thinks of anything except himself. Nico, I don't think they, the Trojans, suspect you; they've seen you running about Troy ever since you could walk. Perhaps you could follow Palamedes without anyone noticing and see what he's up to. Perhaps — sssh! Someone's coming!'

There were footsteps on the stone outside, followed by the hollower thud on the wooden stairs in the tower. Helen sank back into her usual seat by the window and gazed out once more as if nothing mattered but her dreams of distant Lacedaimon, where the city of Sparta stood in the golden light of her recollection above the blue Eurotas that gleamed like no earthly river.

Nico hastily grabbed a set of knuckle-bones and settled himself down in a corner to play, tossing them up and catching them deftly one by one on the back of his hand. He stopped, however, with three of the five already caught, and stared with his best reproduction of childish wonder as the door was flung open and Paris strode in, followed by Palamedes.

'Helen, here's our noble friend Palamedes,' said Paris briefly. 'He's likely to prove the saviour of Troy.'

'Lady Helen,' said Palamedes, bowing elaborately. 'I am delighted to meet you again. Delighted to pay my wespects to the most beautiful woman in all Gweece – no, in all the world. I am delighted, and I think the Twojans are quite wight to fight for you, particuwarly my good fwiend Pawis. I'm so glad to be able to help him against those bwutes of Agamemnon's, most of all Achilles, and Odysseus, and of course your late husband, that oaf Menelaus. But don't worwy, my dear, we'll see to it that you don't have to go back to Gweece with any of them.'

Helen turned. 'Get out of my sight, you treacherous dog,' she said without any passion in her voice, but only a contempt that cut far deeper. 'I know you, Palamedes the sneak, son of Nauplius the wrecker, whom Agamemnon only tolerates among his vassals because his wife Clymene, your mother, is his aunt. If Menelaus were here you would not have dared to speak to the Queen of Sparta as you have done.'

Palamedes flushed crimson, and for a moment Nico thought that he was going to burst into tears like a girl. Instead he shouted, his voice rising to a shrill screech:

'You Spartan cat; you false wunaway, false to one hus-band and weady to be false to another! I'll not forget this insult when the time comes for Menelaus to die, or that imbecile bwat of his over there! You think I'm as silly as any of your high-falutin fwiends fwom Sparta or Argos, do you? Well, before long I'll show you that I'm not!'

Nico was about to spring up and attack Palamedes, but fortunately Paris intervened at that moment.

'You mind your tongue, Helen,' he hissed, his face working with jealous rage. 'You'll not be Queen of Sparta again until we lay it in ruins and hang Menelaus by the heels from the lintel of his own palace for the dogs to tear. And you, Palamedes, pay no attention to her . . . But you'd better not call the Princess of Troy names again, good friend though you are, or I'll be tempted to throw you out of the window to make dog's meat yourself.'

'Pardon me, my dear fwiend,' Palamedes hastened, fanning himself with the corner of his cloak. 'I forgot myself. But don't let's quarwel now. If you wait too long, Achilles may have gone. You have your bow and arwows: it was only the poison you needed . . . Shoot him in the heel: he goes barefoot, but he's wearwing body armour, and gweaves on his legs.'

'Then there's no truth in the story about him being in-vulnerable?' remarked Paris, taking down a stone jar from a high shelf, untying the parchment cover, and dipping the points of his arrows into it one by one.

'Oh, that nonsense about his mother the sea-nymph dipping him in the wiver Styx, but holding him by the heel?' queried Palamedes scornfully. 'I don't believe in any such tales — or in sea-nymphs either. At least I've never seen any . . . But the heel's the safest place, and the poison will stwike up quickly enough.'

'Palamedes!' Helen spoke quietly again, but with a different intensity in her voice. 'Think before you betray Achilles to his enemies. Whatever your father may have been, you were born and bred a Greek. Trojans and other barbarians betray their friends, but *Greeks* don't do such things, nor dishonour the gods like this. Oh, shame! A prince of Argos to betray Achilles, the greatest of all the Greeks, to a barbarian who murders with poisoned arrows one who comes under a vow of safe conduct! What will the minstrels say in the days to come when they sing of the siege of Troy, and the part that Palamedes played in it?'

'They may sing what they like,' snapped Palamedes, though the colour rose to his face again at Helen's words. 'Minstwels sing such awful lies. But I've seen to it that the twuth shall be told: my scwibe Dictys of Cwete is witing an account of the war, a twue historwy which will outlive any lies the minstwels may tell, even if they take bwutes like Achilles or Odysseus as their hewoes ... And talking of witing, weminds me: there's a message I hope to be able to send, can you give me a clay tablet on which to wite it?'

'We don't do much writing in Troy,' said Paris, returning the last arrow to his quiver, 'but there's usually some about in here which the boy plays with. Nicostratus, some clay quickly!'

Looking as stupid and sulky as possible, with a heart beating fast with fear and excitement, Nico shambled forward to a leather bucket under the table and took a lump of moist clay out of it which he put down on top of the table.

Palamedes at once moulded a piece of the soft grey substance into a flat, narrow strip six or seven inches long by less than two wide, smoothed the top of it with his dagger, and began scratching on it quickly and deftly with a long pin that Helen had left lying on the table.

Nico watched curiously as the strange signs took form in two lines running from end to end of the tablet, and wished that he could understand them. True, he had seen Antenor making lists with the aid of just such signs; but very few in Troy could read, and as these were used only by the priests for recording stores or treasures, he had taken no interest.

'There now,' said Palamedes, getting up from the table and holding the tablet carefully in his left hand. 'Ten minutes in the sun will harden that quite enough, and I can do it while I sit on the wall and watch you shoot Achilles as he comes out of the marsh and walks away by the Skaian Gate. He's sure to go that way. No, I'll leave it on the wall, and wun down to send him out of Twoy first: if I don't, he'll go on talking to that pwincess of his until Hecuba comes back, and he'll be swearwing his pwecious oath and being let out of the gates in style like an ally. That would never do! Let's be going.'

Paris led the way out of the room, and Nico half turned to be ready to dash out and warn Achilles the moment they had gone down the wooden stairs. But Palamedes's next words sent a cold dread to his heart.

'Lock and bar the door, Parwis! Surely you don't want Helen or the boy wunning out and spoiling our game!'

'Trust you to think of everything!' laughed Paris.

The heavy wooden bar thudded into place; there was a pause while Paris tied the tough oxhide thongs to hold it in place. Then their footsteps clattered down the stairs, and faded suddenly into the pad-pad of leather on the stone outside.

Nico sprang across the room and pulled desperately at the door. But the thick boards did not even shake, and the narrow slit was far too small for him to get so much as a finger through to reach the thong which could be caught with a key only if left loose and untied.

Chapter 5

THE POISONED ARROW

'Mother! Mother!' cried Nico, his voice breaking as he fought back a sob. 'I can't get out—and Paris has gone to kill Achilles! Palamedes has betrayed him, and even a prick from one of the poisoned arrows will kill him! If only I could get out, I might reach the Temple in time to warn him! Oh, what shall I do?'

'If Paris goes with Palamedes, or watches him from the top of the wall, he'd see you — and probably shoot you with one of his hateful arrows,' said Helen in a dead, hopeless voice. But she was gazing out of the window again, and suddenly she caught her breath.

'Yes!' she gasped, 'they are coming! The whole Greek army is marching against Troy! Oh, if only they get here in time! . . . If only I could climb down and run to them!'

'Perhaps I could?' exclaimed Nico excitedly.

'No, no!' said Helen firmly. 'Even if you got down in safety, they'd kill you before you could tell them who you were or why you came. But you wouldn't even get to them. The archers on the wall would shoot you: you've forgotten that Paris posted them there to shoot either of us if we ever did manage to escape — ever since the time he caught me using that rope you and Polyxena got from the Treasury.'

Nico thought a moment, looking out to the distant line of chariots and men in flashing bronze armour moving slowly across the plain.

'Mother,' he said, quite calmly now. 'If Palamedes goes straight to the Temple – he'll be there by now. And if Achilles goes at once by this secret passage, which must be somewhere in the Temple, he'll be out of Troy before even the chariots arrive. I *must* get out of here. Even if I don't reach the Temple before he goes, I can follow him and catch up with him before he comes out into the open. The marsh, Palamedes said: that's in the hollow on this side of the Skaian Gate. Yes, that's where Paris disappeared so mysteriously when he was fighting in single combat with Menelaus: he turned up in Troy not long afterwards, and said that Aphrodite had carried him away out of danger – but of course he must have come through the passage.'

Now Helen seemed really to wake to the emergency, and she too sped to the door and tried in vain to open it.

'If we shouted,' suggested Nico, 'aren't any of the slave-girls downstairs?'

'No,' Helen answered. 'I sent them all away when I realized that the beggar was really Odysseus. And the only guards who might hear are the archers on the walls, and they've strict orders never to leave their posts.'

'There's old Aethra!' exclaimed Nico. 'Couldn't she understand enough to come and loose the bolt?'

'We could try,' said Helen, 'but I'm sure it's no use. She's quite, quite imbecile now, and just wouldn't understand.'

'Aethra! Aethra!' shouted Nico, and Helen added her voice to his. 'Come here, Aethra, and let us out!'

But the old queen in the little room at the corner of the tower not ten yards away from them remained lost in her world of half a century before, and paid no attention.

'It's useless,' sobbed Helen. 'Nothing of today means

anything to her. She doesn't live in our world any more, but in a world that only she remembers, when Theseus was the young hero who sailed from Athens to kill the Minotaur and rescue the youths and maidens whom Minos of Crete claimed each year as tribute . . . Theseus! Oh, great Zeus! There *is* a chance! Not for nothing did you give me my strange gift of imitating voices!'

Nico knew of Helen's power of mimicry, and had often heard her recapture the voices that should have been so dear and familiar to him, Menelaus and Hermione, Clytemnestra and Agamemnon, Penelope and Odysseus. But now he listened awestruck as Helen called aloud in the slow deep voice of the long-dead hero of Athens.

'Aethra! Aethra my mother! It is I, your son Theseus! Mother, come quickly and let me out of this labyrinth! I have slain the Minotaur, and I have followed the clue of thread which Ariadne the king's daughter set in my hand. But the door of the labyrinth is shut, and I cannot win out of it to save the youths and maidens of Athens and sail home to seek my father Aegeus and become king of all Attica . . . Aethra, my mother, come quickly and save your son!'

Helen paused, and Nico listened breathlessly. Yes! There was the quick shuffle of footsteps outside, and a moment later the tremulous old voice of Aethra came to them, speaking more clearly than Nico had ever heard it.

'Theseus! My darling son! Where are you?'

'Aethra, my mother! In here! Quickly, unbar the door!' The tears were running down Helen's face as she spoke, and she had the utmost difficulty in controlling her voice.

'Yes, yes!' they heard Aethra mutter. 'The bolt is shot, and the thongs are tied. Oh, surely Daedalus himself made such a knot! Athena give me cunning to untie it! Yes, yes, the thongs are coming! Ah, my Theseus, in spite of all the princesses of Crete can do, a mother's hands are best when all's said and done.'

'May the gods forgive me for deceiving her like this!' sobbed Helen under her breath as they heard the bolt slide slowly back.

The door swung open, and Aethra stood there, the little shrunken figure seeming for a moment almost tall, and very regal; the dim old eyes bright with eagerness.

'Theseus, my Theseus — where are you? Surely it was you who called me?' As Nico dived under Aethra's outstretched arm and sped down the stairs, he heard Helen say, as she caught the old queen in her arms, 'Yes, daughter of Pittheus, it was Theseus who called — so that you might save the land of Greece and the bravest of her heroes, just as he saved the land from evil men and his own city from Minos of Crete long ago when all the world was young . . .'

Nico slowed down for a moment as he came out on to the wall where the guard stood just out of sight of the courtyard.

'Ha, the little Greek louse again!' cried the guard. 'I'll show you how we in Troy deal with pests like you!'

He aimed a blow at Nico's legs with the handle of his spear. But Nico sprang nimbly over it, crying, 'Lice can jump higher than fleas, and bite harder too!'

The spear handle crashed against the corner of the steps and split down the length of the shaft. Nico left the guard swearing loudly over the damage, and sped on down the steps into the hot courtyard, across it in the glaring sun, and up the edge of the Temple platform between the columns of the portico.

In the dimly lit kella he found Polyxena kneeling in front of the low altar on which a lamp burnt, while Theano stood beside it dropping grains of incense into the flame and chanting in a low voice after the Oriental fashion usual in Phrygia:

> Pallas, warrior maiden;
>   Pallas, given of Zeus;
> Pallas, with terror laden,
>   With aegis of deadly use.
>
> Pallas, sender of Furies;
>   Pallas, the souls inspire
> Of men, to seek war's fierce glories,
>   Of women —'

'Polyxena! Theano!' Nico broke desperately into the hymn. 'Where's Achilles? Quick! I must stop him!'

'Nicostratus!' Theano's priestly voice might have awed even Paris. 'How dare you burst like this into the sacred Temple of Pallas Athena, into the presence of the very Palladion, and interrupt the divine hymns of her priestess?'

'I came to save Achilles!' gasped Nico. 'Palamedes has betrayed him to Paris who's gone up to the Skaian Gate to shoot him with poisoned arrows when he comes out of the secret passage. For goodness' sake show me the way into it and I'll run down it after him: I may be able to stop him before he comes out into the open.'

'Nico! Oh how awful! Quick, you must save him!' began Polyxena, catching Nico by the arm to lead him into the shrine. But Theano interrupted quickly, still in her voice of awe-inspiring command.

'Polyxena! Remember your oath! I forbid you to show

Nicostratus the most dangerous secret in Troy! You talk of treachery,' she went on, turning to him, 'but who more likely to prove a traitor to Troy than you yourself, the son of our enemy, King Menelaus? As for Palamedes, he is vowed to the service of Troy by oaths that no man would dare to break.'

For the first time a doubt crossed Nico's mind, and he blurted it out aloud, so great was his trouble.

'Then – then the secret treaty with Achilles was all a trick to get him into Paris's power? And you, Polyxena, were helping to cheat him by pretending to be in love with him?'

'No!' Polyxena swung round on him, her eyes flashing and a dagger half drawn in her hand. 'Nico, how dare you, how can you think such a thing? I love Achilles, and he loves me. He has sworn to leave the war for my sake and sail home to Greece with me as his wife.'

'But Paris is at this moment waiting over the Skaian Gate to shoot him as soon as he appears outside the walls,' said Nico slowly, 'and Theano tells me that there has been no treachery. Who am I to believe? All I know is that not a quarter of an hour ago Palamedes and Paris locked me into the tower with Mother and went away laughing together over the cruel death they had planned for the bravest of all the Greeks.'

'It must be true!' cried Polyxena. 'Nico, forgive me – it was natural for you to doubt. So, quick, you must save Achilles. Theano, please show him the way into the –'

'Polyxena, I forbid you to speak!' interrupted Theano fiercely. 'Paris knew of the secret treaty with Achilles, and I do not believe that he would break it so treacherously. No, Nicostratus has invented this story to discover the secret way out of Troy. Yes, of course, Odysseus!

We caught him disguised as a beggar in this very Temple, and my sister the Queen very foolishly let him go — if Helen could get him out of Troy. Obviously she can't, and this is his trick to discover the secret way. Go out of this sacred place at once, Nicostratus, or I will call the guards to bind you until I can tell King Priam of all that has happened.'

There were tears in Nico's eyes as he turned and walked out of the Temple, tears both of grief and rage — he hardly knew which was uppermost. What could he do? he wondered wildly. What *should* he do? He was a Greek trying to help the Greek cause but — the horrid doubt flashed suddenly before him — was he helping them most by saving Achilles who was about to prove false to King Agamemnon and make a separate peace with Troy after vowing to fight until Troy was conquered? Nico stopped dead as he thought of this; but then the thought came once more that he was a Greek, and it was surely his duty at all costs to save a Greek from being murdered by a Trojan — particularly when that Trojan was Paris. As he began to walk across the courtyard Polyxena ran out of the Temple and overtook him.

'Nico!' she gasped. 'I *do* believe you! I don't know what's going on, but I'm sure you're right and that Palamedes is the traitor. I daren't tell you the secret of the way out of Troy, and if I did Theano would stop you from using it. But I'm going to find my mother and tell her what you say. She'll be able to stop Paris if anyone can.'

'Then I'll go up to the wall,' cried Nico. 'I hardly dare to go near Paris at the moment, as he locked me into the tower so that I shouldn't warn Achilles. I wonder where Palamedes is . . . Oh, if only I knew where Odysseus had gone!'

111

Polyxena was already speeding away in search of Hecuba, so Nico dashed up the stone steps on to the wall once more, but instead of going up to Helen's tower he ran along towards the guard-room in the corner near the Skaian Gate, passed it without attracting attention, and made his way to the corner of the wall near the side of the tower. From here he could see round almost to the Skaian Gate, and the tops of the two low towers on either side of it.

The first thing he saw was Paris standing on the nearer tower with his bow in his hand and an arrow already on the string. Looking out over the edge of the wall he could see the Greek army just coming into sight beyond the corner of Helen's tower; and hardly had he seen, when the guards along the wall saw too, and shouted down to the garrison below and behind them.

'To arms, men of Troy! The Greeks are coming to attack the Skaian Gate!'

In a moment the quiet city sleeping in the heat of early afternoon woke into life. Men came running to the open court above the steep, narrow ramp leading down between high walls and through the Skaian Gate; chariots were being pulled out and horses harnessed to them, and the Trojan chiefs such as Aeneas and Deiphobus and young Polites could be seen buckling on their armour, while their squires brought out helmets and spears and swords for them.

Below Helen's tower and partly out of sight round its corner the ground fell away steeply to a green patch of marsh in a hollow like a short tributary to the flat dry stream of the Scamander, and suddenly Nico saw that Paris was looking towards this place, and then slowly raising his bow.

Nico moved along the wall towards the Skaian Gate, trying to see round the corner of Helen's tower. All the guards seemed to have run down to join the throng by the Gate, and Nico moved farther and farther along without realizing it until he was not far from the foot of the steps leading up to where Paris stood with bow half bent.

The Greeks were drawing rapidly nearer; they had almost reached the stony bed of the Scamander. But now Nico could see someone moving in the thick reeds beyond the corner of the tower. Then Achilles appeared, drawing himself up the bank to the hard ground which sloped down gradually to the open space in front of the Skaian Gate, and away to the dried river.

Stepping backwards again Nico bumped into a guard who had not gone down to join the troop which was already moving down the steep, narrow street towards the Gate.

'Great Zeus, for a bow and arrow,' muttered the guard, 'I'd shoot him, if it cost me my life.'

Nico gasped, for the voice was that of Odysseus, and glancing up under the helmet pulled well over the brows he saw that it was indeed he.

'Nicostratus!' Odysseus hissed, recognizing him. 'That's Achilles over there, and that devil Paris is waiting for him with his arrows, with Palamedes the traitor to see foul play . . . Oh gods, that I must see this happen and can do nothing to prevent it. The bravest man, the greatest fighter, the noblest Greek of all to be betrayed like this by that mincing, rotten-hearted sissy Palamedes, and shot down by the vilest barbarian in Troy . . . I'd have gone up and thrown the two of them from the tower, only Paris would have shot me before I was half-way up the steps, and still have shot Achilles . . .

Nicostratus, why in the name of Artemis did you not bring a bow and a quiver of arrows with you?'

Nico saw the knuckles of Odysseus's hands turn white as he gripped the edge of the parapet, and his face looked grey and seamed with pain.

Then the bow twanged above them, and they saw Achilles suddenly stumble forward and fall. In a moment he was up and running across the open. But he was limping, and he reeled as he ran. Then he stopped suddenly, put his hands to his mouth, and cried aloud in the great voice which had so often struck terror into the hearts of all the Trojans, 'To the rescue, leaders of the Greeks! Rescue, Agamemnon, Menelaus, Diomedes, Odysseus! It is I, Achilles, son of Peleus; and I am wounded in the heel by a coward's shot from behind!'

With a roar the Greek chariots flashed forward, and as they did so the Skaian Gates swung open and with an answering roar the Trojans poured out on to the plain. The two forces crashed together round and over the fallen Achilles, and the full din of battle burst suddenly over the quiet world: the cries of men and the screams of horses, the clash and clang of bronze on bronze and the dull thud, thud of wood or stone against leather.

'Only the heel! A wound merely – and he can't shoot again,' gasped Odysseus.

'No!' sobbed Nico wildly. 'The arrow was poisoned, and there is no cure for the poison Paris uses. Oenone the white witch of Ida taught him how to mix it.'

'Then may Paris die in torment, wounded by the arrows Heracles dipped into the Hydra's burning blood!' hissed Odysseus. 'Oh gods, if I win out of Troy, I'll set sail at once to fetch Philoctetes who has those arrows. And as for Palamedes, I'll –'

'Look out!' whispered Nico. 'He's coming!'

With a great effort Odysseus composed himself, stood to attention, and twisted his face suddenly to one side in an effort to disguise himself still more.

Then Palamedes came tittupping down the steep steps from the tower where Paris still stood gloating.

'Ah, guard, you there!' he cried when he saw Odysseus. 'Take this message to the king your master, and tweasure it carefully, for it bwings him the best news he ever heard. I can get out of Twoy with all these Twojan soldiers. But I'll be back again and weport what's happening, and how we may best defeat the plans of those bwutes, Agamemnon and Odysseus.'

So saying, he handed over the clay tablet, now baked hard by the sun, and hastened on down the steps to join the rush through the Skaian Gate.

Odysseus bent over the scratches on the tablet and muttered the words as he spelt them out in the clumsy old Mycenaean alphabet of syllables:

jo a pe do ke   pa ra me de   e ne ka   ku ru so jo

wa na ka te ro jo   a ki ne wa   pa ta jo i

pa ma ko qe   pa ri do

he read: 'For the gold received from you, oh king, I Palamedes have betrayed Achilles to the poisoned arrows of Paris.'

'Yes,' said Odysseus grimly, as he straightened his back and looked down the stairs after Palamedes. 'I will give this to your king, Palamedes the traitor – to your true king whom you would betray to these barbarians as you have betrayed Achilles to his death for gold – or was it for spite?'

Then he turned to Nico and spoke quickly, in a low voice.

'Nicostratus, be sure I shall tell Menelaus of the fine son and the faithful wife he has waiting for him in Troy. I can't say more now; I'm in deadly danger with that murderous bowman still up there, but be sure I'll come again – to speak with you and Helen if I can, and to take the Palladion. Sssh! I must go now: it's too good a chance to miss of getting out in the crowd. And my place is in the battle over the body of Achilles. May the gods be with you!'

Nico leant against the stairs until he saw Odysseus in the street below. Then he turned back to look over the parapet, and in a little while felt sure that the Trojan guard who was working his way deftly round the edge of the battle must be Odysseus.

While he was watching, Paris came strolling down the steps, singing a Greek love-song in a voice of careless glee:

> 'The rose, the crown, the hunter's dart,
> I lay aside: Love rules my heart;
> And far away I fain would dwell,
> With Helen, whom I love so well!'

'Hello, Nico!' he exclaimed. 'Did you see my prize shot? That's finished Achilles! But how did you get here? I thought I'd locked you and Helen up in the tower.'

'Old Aethra untied the bolt and let us out,' answered Nico, not quite knowing what to say.

'What, that crazy old baggage?' cried Paris. 'I'd forgotten all about her. Well, it doesn't matter; you didn't arrive in time to spoil my sport. A good day's shooting I call it. Now I'm off to be congratulated . . .'

Paris went swaggering down the steps, and Nico with a heavy heart made his way up to the Tower where Helen sat by the window looking out at the battle over the body of Achilles, her eyes wide with trouble, and the Star Stone shining like a great wound on her breast.

On the floor, with her head on her lap, lay Polyxena sobbing convulsively, while Helen's long white fingers rested gently on her golden hair.

Chapter 6

THE FALSE PALAMEDES

The battle over the body of Achilles raged all day, and only when dusk was falling did the Greeks drive the Trojans back through the Skaian Gate with loud threats of the most terrible vengeance on man, woman and child when Troy fell. Nico felt that the end must indeed be near; yet, for several weeks, nothing happened.

But on the day that Achilles died, the siege of Troy very nearly came to an unexpected end. Palamedes had judged all Trojans by Paris, the one whom he knew best — and by his own complete selfishness and lack of honour. It never entered his head that Priam would have any scruples over the betrayal of Achilles, or that the gold which the King of Troy had given him could not be earned as well, if not better, by bribing Achilles with Polyxena to retire from the war rather than by causing his death.

Priam, however, was filled with shame at what had happened, and summoning a council of the Trojan chiefs he suggested handing over Paris to the Greeks, or at least banishing him from Troy. But although Antenor openly condemned Paris, and the pious Aeneas shook his head and murmured something about the vengeance of the gods, the rest of the Trojans insisted that all was fair in war, and that Priam and Antenor were old-fashioned in their ideas — which, doubtless, they had learnt from the Greeks themselves, who, as everyone in Troy knew, were complete fools in matters of this kind and had no idea what 'total war' meant.

In fact, the meeting which had been called to condemn Palamedes as a double traitor and banish Paris for having brought an everlasting stain on the honour of Troy, ended in a vote of confidence in Palamedes and another of thanks to Paris, who was hailed tumultuously as the saviour of Troy and an even greater benefactor than Hector had been.

Paris became more and more self-satisfied, and in consequence was kinder to Helen and for a while more tolerant of Nico – who, for his part, took care to keep up the pretence of being still a rather dull and backward child who took no real interest in the events of the war.

He was always wandering about Troy, however, smiling in a puzzled fashion when any Trojan, old or young, jeered or swore at him as a Greek outcast or an enemy spy – but finding in consequence that it was easier and easier to forget that he had ever been in doubt as to which were his own people.

It was mainly Polyxena who had held him to Troy, and after the death of Achilles he scarcely saw her again. For a day or two she spent much of her time with Helen; but after this she more or less said good-bye to both of them.

'I shall do what my father has always wanted,' she said. 'I shall become a priestess, like my sister Cassandra. Now that Achilles is dead I shall never marry, so there is little else that I can do. But oh, I hope that if Troy falls the Greeks will kill me and make an end! I've nothing to live for, and I would ask no better fate than to die on the grave of Achilles!'

So Polyxena went to join Cassandra in the precinct of

Apollo's temple on the other side of Troy, and Nico felt more alone than he had ever done before.

Then Paris seemed on a sudden to become lonely, and his gaiety to sound forced and his boastings an empty mockery.

'He's afraid,' said Helen dreamily, looking out as usual towards the Greek lines, but his time from the roof of the tower which she and Nico had sought for coolness as the sun went down behind Tenedos at the end of a sweltering summer's day.

'Afraid? What of?' queried Nico, watching the little figures in the distance near the Greek encampment and trying to imagine which was his father Menelaus and which was Odysseus.

'The shadow of his death is on him,' said Helen in the same detached voice. 'I think my release is near . . . Great Zeus, if only Menelaus comes quickly!'

'What will happen to us if Paris is killed before the Greeks take Troy?' asked Nico breathlessly.

Helen shivered: 'I am no more here than a captured woman, a slave in all but name . . . According to their barbarous Eastern custom, I shall become the property of one of Paris's brothers: Helenus or – oh gods! – Deiphobus the beast.'

'If only we could escape!' cried Nico desperately. 'This is as bad as the punishment of wicked King Tantalus in the land of the dead – up to the neck in water, and dying of thirst! My father and his people are over there – there where we see them – and we can't get to them!'

'There's no escape,' said Helen. 'Certainly not for me. But when Paris is dead, oh, I'm so afraid for you. They'll all know that the end is near, and fear makes men even crueller than they are already. Sssh! Here comes Paris.'

121

'You've certainly chosen the best place,' Paris exclaimed as he flung himself down near Helen. 'Just the ghost of a breeze. Zeus! I could almost wish for the winter winds from Ida – "Windy Troy" is a myth at this time of year. Curse those Greeks, I wonder what they're up to? There's no news, no real news. What can have become of Palamedes? Perhaps he's gone with Odysseus.'

'What, has Odysseus retired from the war?' asked Helen, trying not to show too much interest.

'No such luck,' growled Paris. 'He's merely gone off on one of his mysterious expeditions, he and Diomedes, in one ship. There's been a great quarrel, and we've lost one of our most dangerous enemies, I'm glad to say. Old Ajax, the son of Telamon, went mad and stabbed himself. The prisoner from whom we got the news said that there was a contest as to who was to have the armour of Achilles: rather a special set, I gather, which those superstitious idiots over there believe was made for him in heaven, by Hephaestus himself. Anyhow that doddering old fool Nestor said it ought to be given to the bravest of all the Greeks. Naturally they couldn't decide that among themselves, so apparently several spies were sent to overhear what *we* thought about it. And they heard a couple of women up on the wall gossiping about the battle in which I killed Achilles. One of them said how brave Ajax was to carry off the dead body; but the other said that was nonsense – she could have carried off the body herself, if she'd been strong enough: the really brave man was Odysseus who held his shield over Ajax while he carried the body into safety. And it's perfectly true: he held up a great shield all the time, so cleverly that I couldn't get an arrow into either of them, try how I might. Anyway Odysseus got the armour, and Ajax went mad

122

with jealousy, tried to finish off Agamemnon and several of the others – without any success, I'm sorry to say – and when he came to his senses was so ashamed that he flung himself on his own sword. Just the silly, pointless sort of thing a Greek would do. Then they had a great funeral for him: not the usual pyre of wood with sacrifices and games, like they had for Patroclus and Achilles, but the sort of funeral he'd have had at home. All because he didn't die in battle. They cut him out a stone coffin underground: I gather that's your barbarous way of doing things in Greece.'

'And what's happened to Palamedes?' asked Helen, ignoring Paris's gibes.

'That's what's worrying us,' Paris continued. 'Our captive didn't know. There seems to have been another quarrel there. Odysseus was always prowling round watching him; and at last he arrested him and brought him before Agamemnon with some tall story that he'd invented. Odysseus always hated Palamedes, and had been trying for years to get rid of him. But we captured our man before the trial had taken place, so all he knew was the merest rumour. It's the same with this business about Odysseus and Diomedes going off in a ship: they were supposed to be sailing as soon as the trial was over. It was apparently due to old Calchas the prophet. He was at his wits' ends to know why Troy hadn't fallen – as if it wasn't obvious that no Greeks could ever get in here! So he keeps thinking up new conditions without which Troy can never be conquered. It was he who started the hare about the Palladion. That seems to have been forgotten now. But the latest ideas are that a son of Achilles must be here, and a fellow called Philoctetes who has the bow and arrows of Heracles.'

'Yes,' said Helen quietly. 'Those arrows were dipped in the blood of the Hydra, and there is no cure for that burning poison . . . One of those arrows will bring death to the man who murdered Achilles; the man who robbed me of my home and caused this war . . . The man whom I hate above all others.'

There was a long silence; and then Paris turned upon Helen furiously, as if to strike her. But something in her eyes stayed his hand. He opened his mouth to curse; but he shut it again without a word. Then he turned and walked in silence to the edge of the roof where the stairs led down on to the wall. Still without a word he swung round suddenly, his sword bare in his hand, and flung it at Nico. Then, without even looking to see if it had found its mark, he clattered down the steps out of sight.

Nico had become so accustomed to avoiding the stones which the Trojan boys had taken to flinging at him, that he dodged the sword without difficulty. Then he picked it up and hid it for future use.

Those were Helen's last words to Paris. He did not come near her tower again, and a week later her prophecy came true. Philoctetes, the greatest archer among the Greeks, arrived at Troy with Odysseus and Diomedes, and on his very first day in battle he wounded Paris in the thigh with one of the arrows of Heracles.

Paris was carried back into Troy, alternately weeping and cursing. All afternoon the most skilful surgeons and physicians toiled over his wound in vain; death crept mercilessly on, and the pain grew fiercer and fiercer.

When night fell a small body of men stole out of Troy by the little eastern gate, carrying Paris on a litter, slipped through the Greek sentinels, and hastened with him towards distant Mount Ida to seek for Oenone the white

witch, the wife whom he had deserted when he carried off Helen from Sparta.

In the morning they came to her cave high up the mountain side, and Paris between his bouts of agony begged her to forgive him, and to cure him of his wound, to do which she alone had the skill.

But Oenone gazed down on him with cold, vacant eyes.

'Ten years ago you deserted me and went to carry off Helen of Sparta,' she said. 'And in a moment of mad jealousy you killed our son Corythus ... Go back to Helen, and let her cure you of your wound.'

Then, without another word, she turned and went into her cave.

So they carried Paris down the mountainside once more; but before they reached the bottom he was dead. Then they heaped a great pyre of wood, placed his body on the top and set light to it. And Oenone, repenting of her cruelty and remembering only the love that had once been between her and Paris, hastened after him to heal his wound – and finding that she was too late, flung herself upon the pyre and died with him.

When she heard of Paris's wound Helen, knowing that there was no cure for it, fled to the house of Antenor, taking Nico with her, and begged for his protection.

'Dear lady,' said old Antenor with his usual grave courtesy, 'I will certainly grant you the protection which this holy Temple and precinct of Pallas gives. Believe me, you are safe enough. Alas that I should say it, but I am sure that Troy is doomed. By the law of Troy you must pass sixty days and nights as a widow before a new husband may take you; and I greatly fear that Troy has not sixty more days before its fall.'

Nevertheless Helen's move proved wise. Not many

days later she was summoned to appear before Priam and the princes in the court of the citadel where important cases were heard and judged.

She and Nico went, accompanied by Antenor and Theano, with a small escort of Temple guards, and found a big gathering awaiting her.

'My daughter,' said old Priam when she appeared. 'I have sent for you to give you, according to our Trojan custom, to your new lord. But whether it shall be Helenus or Deiphobus is yet to be decided.'

Then the two princes set out their cases with much clamour and many angry words. In the end Priam, after long consultation with his advisers, headed by Antenor and Anchises, gave judgement.

'Although Helenus is my eldest surviving son, he is a priest of Apollo and not a warrior. Deiphobus has fought these ten years to keep Helen with us in Troy, therefore he has the greater right to her, and I decree that she is his.'

'If that false judgement holds,' shouted Helenus, 'I renounce you all! I shall leave Troy this very day and go to the Temple of Apollo at Thymbra, with all who care to follow me. As you rightly say, I am a priest: so even the Greeks will respect me and do me no harm.'

And Helenus left Troy immediately, with a small band of attendants – to find that the Greeks did indeed respect him and did him no harm. They did however capture both him and his followers and keep them prisoners for several weeks, though with all honour. And only when they had learnt all that they wished to know did they send Helenus on his way to the Thymbrian temple.

When Helenus was gone, Deiphobus came striding up to Helen with a smile of triumph on his red, bloated face.

'So-ho, my dear, you're mine now!' he cried.

'Not so fast, my lord Deiphobus!' exclaimed Antenor in his deep, solemn voice. 'By our law the lady Helen was your brother Paris's lawful wife. And therefore she is his lawful widow and must remain such in full mourning for her lord for sixty nights and days. She may go safely and freely to her own tower — and trouble her there at your peril!'

'Curse all priests for mischievous trouble-makers!' snarled Deiphobus. And then, with a look of evil glee, he turned to Nico.

'But this Greek cub of my wife's isn't my brother's widow!' he cried. 'And he shall come here and now to serve me — until I get tired of him and kick him from the walls of Troy.'

'Still you go too fast, my lord Deiphobus,' answered Antenor severely. 'And I bid you beware how far you insult the immortal gods by your wicked words and still more wicked deeds. You know well that all the lady Helen's possessions, which include her slaves — and certainly her son — are as inviolate as she is until the sixty days are up. So touch Nicostratus at your peril.'

'All right!' shouted Deiphobus, purple with rage, for never once before had he been thwarted in his desires, however evil. 'Have it your own way until these days are up. But on the sixtieth day I'll tear this young cub limb from limb with my own hands, and drag Helen by the hair from one end of Troy to the other, to show who's master. And when I'm king of Troy, don't expect to receive any gifts for your Temple from me. Indeed I think that there will be a new high priestess on my coronation day. And the husband of the *ex*-priestess has of course none of the rights and privileges which he now enjoys!'

'Many things may happen before the sixty days are ended,' said Antenor quietly, 'and many more before you become king of Troy – a position which I do not think that you will ever hold.'

'Prophesying evil again, you old traitor!' shouted Deiphobus. 'You've been at it since before the war began, when you prevented Paris and me from dealing with Menelaus and Odysseus when they came whining here for Helen to be given back to them.'

'Antenor speaks the truth!' the clear icy voice of the priestess Cassandra cut suddenly across the hot passions of that room like a breath of deadly cold from Ida in mid-winter. 'Troy is doomed! Is doomed! Troy is destroyed by the hands of her own sons, by the hand of Paris the firebrand, and by the hand of Deiphobus who knows no honour and respects no woman. The great beast is already born who shall trample Troy under foot, and never in life shall Deiphobus nor any man have the golden Helen save Menelaus alone. Troy is doomed! Weep, women of Troy, who shall be sold into slavery and to shame and to death! Weep, for your doom is upon you! Your doom and my doom: the axe is already sharpened for me in Mycenae; the knife is whetted for Polyxena on the tomb of Achilles; the child of Hector shall never learn to speak his father's name; the last king of Troy sits upon the throne ... Weep, people of Troy, for the fire is kindled and the swords are sharp that shall destroy us all. Weep! Weep for Troy!'

The cold clear voice had risen and risen, growing more and more shrill and piercing until with the last wild scream Cassandra sank to the floor, foaming at the mouth, and lay without speech or conscious movement.

'Poor child, poor child,' sobbed Hecuba, bending over

her. 'She is mad. The curse of Apollo is strong upon her and makes her speak these words of utter madness.'

Although they might not believe her words, Cassandra's outburst cast a gloom over all in the assembly. Even Deiphobus went without another word, and Antenor escorted Helen and Nicostratus back to the tower in silence.

At the foot of the steps he paused: 'Lady Helen,' he said, 'I believe that you and your son are safe until the sixty days are up. If Troy still stands at the end of that time, I will do what I can for both of you, though it may not be much. But until then my advice to you is that you remain, both of you, in this tower, or go nowhere else except to the Temple of Pallas or to my house behind it.'

When they were alone in the room, Helen gave way to despair. 'I don't mind so much for myself,' she sobbed. 'I suppose I ought to be used to it. The gods made me too beautiful, so that men seem always to be wanting to carry me off: Theseus, and then Paris, and now Deiphobus. If only I knew that Menelaus understood that I love him and him alone, always, whatever happens . . . But I'm afraid, desperately afraid for you, Nico. If the worst comes to the worst, surely Antenor will hide you. Or go to Polyxena and Cassandra, surely they won't let their mad beast of a brother harm you. But oh, if Menelaus would only come — if Menelaus would only come!'

But once again the Greeks showed themselves strangely reluctant to attack. True, they besieged the citadel so thoroughly now that no one could by any means get in or out. But only once was there anything approaching a battle, and that was when an unexpected ally arrived for Troy in the person of Eurypylus, Prince of Cilicia, who came suddenly with a small band of warriors and won right to the Skaian Gate before the Greeks closed in and annihilated his men, young Neoptolemus the son of Achilles, a boy of little more than Nico's age, killing Eurypylus himself in single combat.

When it was realized who the strangers were, Aeneas and Deiphobus led the Trojan forces out to help Eurypylus; but Odysseus and Diomedes at the head of their men drove them back and were only just prevented from following them right into Troy.

Otherwise more than forty of the sixty days of Helen's official widowhood passed with no event of any interest. Each day Deiphobus came, morning and evening, to visit his prisoners in Helen's tower; and although he made no attempt to touch either of them, he seldom came or went without a word or two which brought a flush of loathing and disgust to Helen's face, and a cold fury to Nico that was quite new to him. He had hated Paris, but he hated Deiphobus a hundred times more, and with a new, fierce hatred that sometimes rather frightened him.

'If nothing happens by the fifty-ninth night,' he said quietly to Helen, 'I'll kill him when he comes for the last time. I have Paris's sword hidden among the clothes and sheepskins in the chest.'

But late in the afternoon of the forty-third day quick, unfamiliar footsteps sounded suddenly on the wooden stairs, and the door opened to admit – Palamedes.

There was a moment of horrified silence, and then as Nico moved round towards the chest where Paris's sword was hidden, Helen said, 'Traitor and murderer, what are you doing here? How dare you come into my presence! Oh, if I were a man I'd take you and fling you out of that window to be food for the dogs and vultures.'

'Ah, dear lady Helen,' purred Palamedes in his

stickiest, oiliest tones, 'how can you be so perfectly howid to me? Achilles was a twaitor to Gweece, as well as a danger to Twoy, and it was quite wight of Parwis to destwoy him.'

There was a pause, and then Helen said quietly, but a smile curling her lips, 'Very nearly perfect, my dear Odysseus — but you forget the strange power of mimicry which the gods have given me.'

'On the contrary,' answered Odysseus in his own voice, lowering the embroidered mantle which Nico now noticed he had been holding so as to cast a shadow over the lower part of his face. 'I did not for a moment expect to deceive you once I opened my mouth; but I wanted the expert's opinion on my performance.'

'I'm sure no one in Troy would suspect you,' said Helen, and she laughed for the first time for forty-three days. 'But Odysseus, Odysseus, you can't think how glad we are to see you. Our time was almost up. Do say that you come to set us free, or to tell us that the great attack is about to begin.'

'The fall of Troy is, I believe, very near indeed,' answered Odysseus quietly, 'though my scheme, our scheme, is dangerous — yes, desperate, and it may fail even now. It's almost ready, and I must beg you to help us by staying here . . . But what do you mean by saying that your time is almost up?'

Helen told him briefly but fully all that had happened since the death of Paris, and of the fate that awaited them on the sixtieth day.

'The fifty-ninth night. Hmm!' Odysseus pondered for a moment. 'That's the seventeenth night from now, counting tonight as the first of the seventeen . . . Yes, that's just possible. Look, Helen, it's a risk, but we must take it. On the morning of the seventeenth day from now — that's the last day of your Trojan widowhood — you'll wake to find our camp a heap of ruins, our ships and the whole army gone. But — guard this with your lives, both of you: die any death, meet any fate rather than betray me, and all the kings of Greece — after dark that night we shall return. It's the dark of the moon, praise be to Artemis, otherwise it would be too dangerous. We have our way into Troy — arranged. But we may not be able to find Troy. That's where you come in. A bright lamp in that window is all that the army needs; and you must set it there and make sure that it burns clearly and steadily all night. Then, stay here until Menelaus comes — and you will have done your part.'

'And you'll come in by the secret way — enough of you to open the gates?' queried Helen.

'No,' answered Odysseus shortly. 'That way's too risky. It comes out in the Temple of Pallas, and after I've gone tonight, taking the Palladion with me, they're sure to stop it up, or guard it. Anyhow it leads into the Temple, as I say — and we mightn't get out of the precinct and down to the Skaian Gate. No, my plan's better. But I'd be wiser not to tell you what it is.'

'You don't think we'd betray you, like Palamedes?' cried Nico hotly.

'You might,' said Odysseus grimly, 'under torture. And what you don't know you can't betray.'

'But Palamedes,' exclaimed Nico, following a new line of thought. 'He knows the other way into Troy, and he might betray you.'

'The last thing he betrayed *was* the way into Troy through the drain under the Temple of Pallas,' said Odysseus, 'and it's the last thing he will ever betray.

Yes, he's dead: the army stoned him to death, threw him into an old well and filled it to the top with stones. But, traitor though he was, he was a braver man than ever I dreamt he could be. Well, he was a Greek, and that counts in the supreme moments of life – and death.'

'You took that message to Agamemnon?' queried Nico.

'Yes,' answered Odysseus with a grim smile. 'He said, "Take that to the king" – and I did: to *his* king. Even so he braved it out, and swore that I'd forged the message. Then the gold was dug up under his hut, which ought to have settled it: but he swore I'd had it buried there. However, Achilles *was* dead, and killed by one of Paris's poisoned arrows, and the army believed me and accepted the evidence. Palamedes wouldn't admit his guilt, even at the end, and even then put on a great act of innocence, exclaiming: "Truth, I weep for you. For you have been slain first, and now I follow you to the grave." That convinced his brother Oeax anyhow, and he's sailed back to Nauplia, breathing threats of vengeance, particularly against me. Depend upon it, I shall go down to fame as the villain of the piece, who brought about an innocent man's death by my infernal wiles, because of the grudge I bore him for seeing through my pretended madness when I tried to get out of coming to the war. I didn't improve my chances, either, by keeping my evidence by me for over a week, and watching Palamedes until he set out very early one morning for the marsh down there. I followed him and caught him actually in the drain. He tried to pretend he was merely spying on Troy, just as I had done when I came in as a beggar; and he showed me the mechanism for opening the grid in the Temple . . . Look out! I hear footsteps! Can I hide anywhere, or will it be all right if Palamedes is alone here with you?'

'No it won't!' gasped Helen. 'It's Deiphobus on his evening visit. Where — oh, the chest!'

Nico had already flung it open and was lifting out an armful of fleeces. Swiftly Odysseus sprang in and lay down at full length. Nico arranged the sheepskins over him and lowered the lid gently. Then he snatched up his knuckle-bones and began playing with them on top of the chest itself as Deiphobus strode into the room.

'Ah, the cub playing with bones!' he sneered. 'Eighteen days from now his own bones will be ready for cubs to play with. Suppose we make a cup out of his skull, and then, Helen, you can pledge me in it at our wedding — kiss him goodbye, before you kiss me, don't you know!'

As they had agreed, neither Helen nor Nico paid the slightest attention to Deiphobus, who continued with crueller and cruder jokes and suggestions for several minutes before concluding with a snarl, 'I've some news that may interest you. Palamedes has been murdered on false evidence given by Odysseus. But they didn't all believe that foul Ithacan liar; many of them, headed by a man called Sinon, tried to save Palamedes, and there's been a bigger quarrel than ever before. Our spies overheard a couple of soldiers discussing it all: apparently nearly half the Greek leaders believe Palamedes was innocent and demand the death of Odysseus, or that he should be driven out of the camp. There's a good chance of a real split among them, and if so, we've won the war . . . So you'd better make up your mind to be a good wife to me, for you'll never see Menelaus again!'

Helen still remained silent, and Deiphobus swore at her viciously before going out and slamming the door after him.

When his footsteps had died away in the distance, Nico opened the chest and helped Odysseus out of it.

'I hope I may never have to hide under a sheepskin again!' he gasped, mopping his face, 'I've never been so hot in my life . . . Helen, I don't like that new husband-to-be of yours at all, and you may depend upon us on the seventeenth night from now.'

'Was there any truth in what he said about the quarrel over the death of Palamedes?' asked Helen anxiously.

Odysseus grinned. 'That's what his spies overheard, right enough,' he said. 'And that's just what I wanted them to overhear. My cousin Sinon's a good man, and a brave one too. If Troy falls seventeen nights from now, it will be largely owing to him.'

'We won't be disturbed again,' said Helen. 'So sit down comfortably and have some wine and cakes. And tell us more about your plans. But talk quietly in case any of the sentinels hear you, or one of the slave-girls.'

'Well, I must stay until it's dark,' answered Odysseus, settling himself in Helen's chair by the window. 'After my narrow escape last time I don't go near that Palladion by daylight. Of course I could have taken it, and gone back into the drain at once, but I wanted to speak to you — and to do a little spying.'

'You still think it's worth all this risk to get the Palladion?' asked Helen.

'More so than ever,' replied Odysseus, sipping the sweet Pramnian wine with great relish. 'I tell you, not one of our men will set foot inside Troy while it's here. Calchas has so filled their heads with it, that they all believe that Troy can never be conquered while it's inside the walls. And your Trojan prophet Helenus whom we — well, delayed, on his way to Thymbra, said exactly the same thing. He called it "The Luck of Troy", and the name's caught on all over the camp. So I must steal the Luck of Troy, or all our schemes are useless.'

Night fell while Odysseus talked; and though he told them nothing more of his plans for taking Troy, he kept them enthralled with his tales of the Greek heroes, more particularly the doings of those who lay encamped before Troy. Suddenly Nico felt that he knew them: Philoctetes the tall, silent archer with the limp; slow-speaking, slow-thinking Diomedes, the greatest warrior among them, now that Achilles and Ajax were dead; Aias, son of Oileus, with the wild, violent temper who cared neither for man nor god; young Neoptolemus, who was Achilles all over again but with few brains and not a shred of imagination; soft-voiced, gentle-handed Machaon, the great physician; Echion, famed for his rashness, who, said Odysseus, always leaped before he looked; King Agamemnon, always ready to see an affront to his dignity, but never ready to make up his mind; and Menelaus the king of Sparta, Nico's own father, young and eager in spirit, the best of friends, though not always the wisest of generals. They all came to life and seemed to move visibly before his mind's eye as Odysseus described each of them and sketched them in with anecdotes and a few graphic words.

Suddenly he stopped, and Nico sat back almost with a gasp.

'It's time for deeds now!' he said with a smile. 'Perhaps you'd both better come with me, in case of accidents. Now they know that Palamedes is dead, I may have need of your gift of voices, Helen, and of your speed of foot, Nico.'

So, wrapped in cloaks, they stole quietly down to the

Temple, walking round the edge of the courtyard to avoid the light of the full moon as much as possible. All seemed safe and silent as they came into the kella where the lamp burnt on the altar, lighting up the Temple far more brightly than in the daytime.

'From this side you press that mark half-way down the back of the altar,' whispered Odysseus. 'Look!'

He put his finger on the spot, and the big stone grid fell open with a low thud, leaving a hole two foot square in the floor.

'Goodbye then,' said Odysseus. 'Remember my words. Now I'll get the Palladion from the plinth in the shrine there — Great Zeus, what does this mean?'

The light of the lamp shone clearly into the shrine and lit up the plinth on which the Palladion stood. But it was an empty plinth: the Luck of Troy had gone.

Chapter 7

HELEN'S CHOICE

In his amazement Odysseus sprang into the shrine of the Temple of Pallas, with Nico close behind him. As he stepped out of the way of the lamplight from the altar in the kella he saw Theano standing in the corner with the Palladion in her hands, while Antenor stood on the other side of the plinth carrying what seemed to be a child wrapped in a long dark cloak. In the shadows on either side of them stood Temple guards with drawn swords in their hands.

'Odysseus of Ithaca!' said Antenor in his slow, impressive voice. 'Did you really think that we of Troy were so foolish? Even if Palamedes were not dead, do you suppose that we could put any trust in a traitor – one who had already betrayed the Greeks, his own people? Did you really think that you could come into Troy by this secret way which, for our very necessity, we showed to Palamedes, without us knowing? Surely the wisest of all the Greeks is more foolish than a simple Trojan priestess and her husband!'

'Lord Antenor,' said Odysseus quietly, 'I own myself beaten. For youth, or even middle age, must always be beaten in the end by the wisdom of years. Nevertheless you, who saved Menelaus and myself from the treachery of Paris and Deiphobus, you who have never feared to declare that the cause of Troy is wrong, and the cause of Greece is right – will you not let me go this time, taking with me either that Palladion which the priestess Theano holds in her hands, or else the lady Helen, rightful wife of Menelaus King of Sparta? You are a just man, juster than any of the Trojans: say, will you not let me take my due and go?'

It was a forlorn hope, and Odysseus knew it as he edged nearer to the drain, ready to spring into it and run for his life when all else failed. But he nearly fell, rather than jumped into it when Theano said, 'King Odysseus, Trojans though we are, we know that your cause is right. Therefore when Troy falls, have us in mind and save us from the vengeance of the Greeks. Promise but this, and I will here and now hand over to you the Palladion, the very Luck of Troy, which I hold now in my hands.'

'Lady Theano,' answered Odysseus, his voice shaking with a mixture of doubt, surprise and eagerness, 'I swear to you by my lady Athena who rules all my ways; yes, and if you will by the dread oath of Styx which even the gods themselves dare not break: I swear that you and all your house shall remain untouched when Troy falls. Only remain inside it and hang a leopard skin over the door, and not a Greek shall so much as enter.'

'Good,' said Theano. 'Then I will give this Palladion into your hands. But go at once, and do not seek to return. For know that henceforth this way shall be blocked with a great stone, and guarded by armed men night and day.'

She paused; and Helen, who had been looking earnestly from one to the other and listening to the tones of their voices with a strange, expectant eagerness, uttered a low cry. Then, as all turned towards her, she raised her arm and struck the single lamp on the altar so that it flew like a shooting star into the square hole in the pavement and was extinguished in the moving water at the bottom of it.

There was a moment of silence and stillness in which Nico felt someone brush suddenly past him. Then came smothered exclamations, and he heard Theano's voice say in a little above a whisper, 'He's gone, Antenor! Quick, give me the true Palladion to set once more on the plinth whence it has never stirred till now, Troy's hour of trial, since Pallas Athena flung it from heaven to mark the very heart of Ilion.'

There was another movement in the darkness, an exclamation, and Theano's voice came again, but louder this time.

'Antenor! Antenor! Who spoke? Ah, there you are! A light, bring a light quickly!'

Someone ran against Nico: there was a grunt and a splash. Then Odysseus said quietly from somewhere below in the darkness:

'I thank you, voice of Theano, for placing the very Palladion in my hands.'

As he spoke there was a sudden light as Deiphobus dashed into the Temple carrying a flaming torch. For a moment Nico saw; and the scene fixed itself in his mind: Helen in front of the plinth with a strange look of triumph on her face, Antenor and Theano on either side, a little behind her, both it seemed with their hands stretched out on either side of the plinth – on which to his amazement the strange, misshapen stone that was called the Luck of Troy stood as it had always done.

Then he sprang back to avoid Deiphobus who struck at him with the torch, and heard Odysseus shout from below, 'Quick, Helen and Nico! Down into the drain if you can!'

Like a flash of light Helen eluded both Antenor and Theano and sprang down through the square hole in the floor. Nico tried to follow, but Deiphobus struck him to the ground, and whipping out his sword held it to Nico's throat, crying as he did so, 'Helen, come back, or I'll kill Nicostratus! By Hades, I'll cut his throat over the edge of the altar as if he were a sheep and drench you below there in his life-blood!'

'Go on, mother, I'd rather die!' shouted Nico hysterically. 'Tell Menelaus that I gave my life to save you from Deiphobus. He'll kill us both, otherwise.'

In the moment of intense silence that followed, the voice of Odysseus came clearly to those in the Temple as he said quietly to Helen, 'What he says may be true. For your own sake, for the sake of Menelaus, of Hermione, of us all — come quickly!'

'No, no!' wailed Helen. 'Don't strike, Deiphobus, I'm coming back. Go quickly, Odysseus, you tempter. Tell Menelaus why I stayed.'

Helen's head and shoulders appeared in the opening, and with a savage laugh of triumph Deiphobus seized her and dragged her roughly back into the Temple.

'Now then!' he shouted. 'Who's going down there ferreting after Odysseus? I'll give two slave-girls and a helmet full of gold to whoever brings back the head of that dog-fox!'

Two of the guards started forward; but Antenor motioned them back.

'You'd never catch him,' he said, 'and once out of the drain he's more than a match for them, even if there's no one waiting for him out there. No, close the grid, and place two great blocks of stone over it. Then come away from it and listen to me . . . You see that the very Palladion stands safely here in the shrine where it has always stood? Well, Theano and I knew that Odysseus would

come again to steal it, and so we were ready for him . . .
He thinks that he has stolen the Luck of Troy, and is
carrying it with him now. But what he has is a mere copy
which we made ready, and which my wife placed in his
hands.'

'Trust a priestess to cheat a thief!' laughed Deiphobus. 'But guard the real Palladion well, nevertheless – and this fox-hole. Now then, men, drag these two away, my false wife and this treacherous Greek cub . . . All right, Antenor, I haven't forgotten: it's still seventeen days before I can thrash my wife and hang my step-son by the heels from the walls of Troy. But until then, I'll see to it that they're locked up safely; and as all of us in Troy are getting short of food, it's only right that these two should set a good example by going on half rations.'

The next two weeks passed like a nightmare. There were guards outside Helen's tower – in the courtyard, on the walls, at the foot of the stairs, on the stone steps. Deiphobus visited them at unexpected moments both by day and night, as well as his official inspections morning and evening; and never without some coarse gibe at Helen and some diabolical suggestion of the torture and death in wait for Nico.

A detailed search of the room robbed Nico of the sword, as well as of any garment, skin rug and even tapestry that could by any possibility be made into a rope to be used for escape.

Again and again Nico considered the chances of climbing down the wall below the window: but, even to his fear-sharpened mind, he was forced to admit that any such attempt meant certain death. For the sill of the window-place stuck out at least a foot, and the wall below it was a thirty-foot perpendicular of smoothly-hewn stone carefully set and so well mortared that neither a toe nor a finger could be inserted between any of them. Below the sheer drop of thirty feet the wall slanted outward steeply for another twenty, and was set on solid rock sloping away with sharp cracks and uneven fissures to the edge of the shallow valley with the treacherous green marsh into which the drain from the citadel flowed out.

Helen and Nico, after Deiphobus had left them on their first night of captivity, had seen two dark figures stealing out of the marsh nearly a quarter of a mile away, and had guessed by the load on his back that one of them was Odysseus. The other, they learnt afterwards, was Diomedes, who had waited to guard his line of retreat.

'If only we could call to him!' murmured Helen.

'He might hear, even from there,' suggested Nico.

'No,' Helen exclaimed hastily. 'It would mean his certain death. The guards on the wall at either side of the tower are armed with bows; and you may be sure their arrows are poisoned. And even if we could speak with Odysseus, I don't know what to tell him. Has he got the true Palladion or the false one? Is he deceived or is Theano? I guessed in that moment in the Temple that what she held out to him must be a forgery, and that what Antenor held under his mantle was the Palladion itself. In the darkness I stepped to where I thought he was and spoke to him with the voice of Theano . . . Someone gave me an image: I gave it to someone. I can only pray the gods that it was the right image and that it was to Odysseus that I gave it.'

'Theano thinks the image still in the Temple's the true Palladion,' said Nico. 'What will happen if Odysseus has the false one? After all, that's how Theano and Antenor meant it to be.'

'I doubt whether Odysseus really believes in the Luck of Troy,' said Helen shivering, 'and I don't know what to think. Theano believes in it utterly, and so does everyone here . . . Surely they can't all be wrong? . . . If Odysseus has the false Palladion, and thinks it's the real one, he'll carry out his plan for the capture of Troy — and fail. If he discovers it's a forgery, and he may if Helenus is still a prisoner in the Greek camp, no one will dare to attack. Then another attempt will have to be made to steal the real Luck of Troy. No one but Odysseus will dare to do it — and he can hardly hope to escape a third time.'

'He may have the real Palladion after all,' said Nico hopefully.

'But if not,' went on Helen, her eyes large with trouble, 'you and I are doomed. He'll not be able to steal the true Palladion in time to carry out the attack on the seventeenth night, and if they try without the Luck of Troy, I'm sure they won't succeed in taking the city. Oh, if only we knew!'

'I'm sure I could tell which Palladion it was,' said Nico hopefully.

'Perhaps,' answered Helen. 'But from what Deiphobus said, I'm sure we are both strict prisoners here.'

'But Theano and Antenor will know,' exclaimed Nico desperately.

'If they've no reason to doubt, they won't examine the thing,' said Helen. 'And I feel sure they believe that Odysseus has the forgery. Anyhow, I don't suppose we'll see either of them.'

Helen was right. Except for Deiphobus no one else came near them. Even the slave-girls were replaced by two dusky-skinned women belonging to Deiphobus, who appeared to be deaf and dumb, and might well have been so.

The hours seemed to pass with leaden slowness — but the days to rush by with a sickening and increasing speed. Nico, alternately filled with hope and despair, saw silver hairs come suddenly among the gold on Helen's head as she sat hour after hour gazing wide-eyed out of the window towards where Menelaus was.

The sixteenth day since Odysseus had been with them came and faded into darkness, and Deiphobus exulted and licked his thick lips like a beast of prey that scents blood.

'You will see the sun set tomorrow, Nicostratus, but you will never see it set again!' he cried. 'You may bless the sun at its rising tomorrow, but the next day you will be cursing it in your agony while you writhe and roast in its beams as you hang head downwards against the outer wall striving in vain to shield your bleeding flesh and your blinded eyes from the flies and the birds of Troy, who know how to treat a treacherous Greek cub. And maybe I'll find time after my marriage feast in the evening to cut you down so that the dogs may enjoy what's left of you.'

'The gods of Greece will not allow such wickedness,' said Helen rising suddenly to her full height, her eyes flashing and her breast heaving until the Star Stone shone and glimmered in the evening light and once again the blood-drops seemed to drip and fall from it. 'Apollo and Poseidon have shaken the dust of Troy from their garments and turned away from the walls which they built in the ancient times. Athena averts her eyes from the suppliants who kneel before her image. This city of evil and cruelty and broken faith is doomed.'

In the silence that followed, like an inspired echo to her words, came, small and distant, the sound of Cassandra's voice from somewhere far down in the heart of Troy.

'Weep, daughters of Ilion, for the Luck of Troy is departed.

148

'Cry, Trojans, cry, for your doom draws near. Sleep all those who may, for you shall soon sleep indeed.'

For a moment Deiphobus was frightened, and he cowered back making the sign with his fingers which is used in the East to avert the Evil Eye.

Then he burst out into curses once more, on women prophets of evil in general, and on Helen and Cassandra in particular.

'As for your Greeks,' he ended up, 'they are already rotting by their rotten ships. Since we killed Achilles they haven't dared to attack us. Depend upon it, that coward Agamemnon is planning to lead a general panic in the direction of Greece. There's civil war among them over the murder of Palamedes; and in this heat the plague is killing them by the dozen. Only those sentinels and guards round the walls are still carrying on the war, and they're the picked followers of Odysseus and Menelaus. Wait until the first rains come, and we'll slaughter them all, and chase the remnant in their rotten ships – and I hope they sink! You won't live to see that, Nicostratus; but Helen will.'

Deiphobus went fuming out of the room, pausing only to shut and bar the door, and his footsteps died away in the distance.

Darkness fell over Troy, and Nico tried to sleep, but only seemed to grow more and more awake as the hopeless hours drained away his courage, leaving only the empty terror of the new reality which was rushing to meet him – Death.

He had seen men die: he could not have lived through the brutal ten years of the siege of Troy without meeting death and suffering again and again. But this was something quite new: Death was coming for him. This was no

149

flirtation with death of a man going out to the fierce excitement of battle in the expectation of conquest.

Nico writhed and bit his cloak to keep himself from screaming out loud. What would it be like? Strange, forced pictures flitted in front of his mind's eye: darkness; the funeral pyre; the vaguely imagined Land of the Dead – the black river of Styx, Charon with his grim boat, Hades sitting in judgement, twilight fields of asphodel – Hector, Achilles there already. Troilus, Priam's golden boy, who had gone out with a smile on his lips and his eyes large with wonder, and been brought back to Troy a white and broken body that meant – nothing.

Nico slept, and his dreams were strangely untroubled. But he woke in the very depths of the night to hear unaccountable sounds floating across the distance on the north-west wind.

He lay for a little while trying to imagine what they were. The sounds came from across the plain where the Greek camp had stood for as long as he could remember. Perhaps they were preparing a great attack; perhaps those sounds were the thousands of the Achaians, of *his* people, bearing ladders to scale the walls of Troy and set him and Helen free.

Eagerly he sprang up and ran across to the window. It was quite dark outside, and there was no moon. But beyond the plain by the edge of the sea a great fire was burning, and tiny black figures were running about in front of it; while beyond it, when the smoke blew aside for an instant, he could see ships with sails already set.

Down below, near the wall of Troy, the watch-fires marking the guard-posts of the besieging force burnt redly as usual; but there seemed to be no movement about any of them. Nico turned back into the room, wondering

if this too was a dream. Helen moaned in her sleep as she moved uneasily on her couch. He gathered his cloak round him, for the chill before the dawn was stealing up from the sea, and lay down again to think it all out . . .

He was woken suddenly by a confused babel of voices and – he rubbed his ears as well as his eyes – the wild notes of the Phrygian flute and the glad clash of cymbals and drums.

Springing up, he went to the door and could hear the

voices more clearly, and catch like a refrain running behind all the sounds the one clear rhythm of words: 'The Greeks have gone! The Greeks have gone!'

Nico heard and repeated the words to Helen who had woken as he sprang across the room. Together they ran to the window and looked out.

'It's true!' gasped Nico. 'They've gone! They've all gone!'

Below the wall the watch-fires still smouldered, but there were no Greek sentinels standing or sitting about them. And far away across the plain where the huts and the stockade had stood for so long was only a line and heap of smoking ruins. No ships were drawn up on the shore beyond, and there was not even a sail to be seen on the sea, pale blue and misty in the morning light.

'They've gone,' said Helen with a little gasp. 'Will they return as Odysseus promised? Can they return tonight, before it's too late? And how, oh, how does he plan to get into Troy and open the gates if my lamp guides the army back in the darkness? . . . And if they do not come tonight, my lamp will not shine again in this window to guide them when they do return to Troy.'

Chapter 8

THE NIGHT OF DOOM

That day Troy went mad. But Helen and Nicostratus were kept out of the turmoil, and only heard about what was going on from Deiphobus who visited them from time to time, more and more drunk on each occasion.

Drink seemed to be flowing freely throughout Troy, and all the reserves of wine were broached and drunk unmixed by the happy throngs; while down on the plain huge fires were lighted to cook oxen and sheep left behind by the Greeks, and the Trojans, who had been on the edge of starvation for several months, gorged themselves with roast meat.

'The Greeks have gone all right,' Deiphobus assured his two prisoners. 'We've scared those rats away at last. They've left nothing behind except these sheep and oxen – and the bones of many dead men, I'm glad to say. Oh yes, they've left one curiosity, down over there by the sea: a huge, wooden image of a horse. It's an offering to Poseidon, the Lord of Horses, for a safe passage back to Greece: I hope our Lord the Earth-shaker sinks the whole lot of them! He ought to, as we're bringing that horse up into Troy, however big it is. Both Calchas and Helenus seem to have agreed that Poseidon would only accept the offering if it was too big to be brought into Troy. Of course Priam and Antenor wanted to have it burnt; and that pious donkey my cousin Aeneas, after a lot of hard thinking came out with one of his usual wise remarks:

"The Greeks are most to be feared when they give us gifts!" That was the best he could manage, and they very nearly had their way, because old Laocoon the mad priest agreed with them, and went round repeating what Aeneas had said. But I'm glad to tell you that when he went down to look at Poseidon's shrine under those rocks over there on the coast — and he hadn't been able to go there for years, owing to the Greeks — he found a fine large octopus in possession, and, being quite insane, attacked it single-handed, or with only a couple of boys to help him, and came to a sticky end.'

'And the horse is coming into Troy?' asked Helen. 'How did you discover what it was for?'

'Oh yes, it's coming!' said Deiphobus complacently. 'I'm really ruler of Troy now, whatever my father says, and however grim and disapproving Antenor looks. That octopus turned the scales anyway. A lot of fools started shouting that Poseidon was angry with Laocoon, and had sent the creature on purpose. And as for knowing what the horse was for, we happen to have some reliable information.

'We'd hardly got down to the camp and found the horse when my men came across the one Greek who'd been left behind — a fellow called Sinon who seems to be some sort of cousin of Odysseus, and hates the old Ithacan fox nearly as much as I do. After that trouble over the murder of Palamedes this Sinon apparently accused Odysseus of forgery — writing the tablet himself, and hiding the gold and everything, just to get Palamedes stoned. Of course no one dared suggest that Odysseus was the one to stone, and as no one liked Palamedes very much it was obvious what the general vote would be. Odysseus didn't appear to bear any grudge to Sinon; but before the Greeks set sail Calchas declared that one of their number must be sacrificed. He reminded them that the first Greek to land was destined to meet an untimely end — that tall fellow Protesilaus whom Hector killed in the very first battle. So he said a Greek must die as the ships sailed away — a noble Greek. The lot fell on Sinon, Odysseus saw to that; and he also saw to it that Sinon was flogged unmercifully when he tried to bring up the Palamedes business again. Sinon got away, however; he broke his bonds when they were dragging him to sacrifice during the night; and he hid in the filthiest mud-hole on the plain — a place where the Greeks had dumped refuse and offal for years. He was so furious about it all, and particularly with Odysseus, that he told us about the horse without any persuasion . . . Well, without very much persuasion: we hadn't really done more than put a sword into the fire to heat, and got a bow-string into position round his head.'

'Trust a Trojan barbarian to use torture if he gets a chance,' exclaimed Helen, turning away in disgust.

'I suppose you Greeks always treat your enemies well?' sneered Deiphobus. 'What about Ixion and his red-hot stones?'

'A good example,' said Helen quietly. 'Zeus showed what he thought of Ixion: haven't you heard that he swings for ever on a burning wheel in Tartarus, the place of the damned? I wonder what punishment Zeus has in reserve for you?'

'Well, I'll do something to deserve it tomorrow!' cried Deiphobus with a look at Nico. 'I must go and super-intend the bringing in of the horse. You'll see it from here. I'll come back later and tell you what's happening.'

Deiphobus strode rather unsteadily out of the room,

and Helen returned to the window, where Nico joined her with beating heart and hope struggling with fear.

'What does it all mean?' he asked breathlessly. 'It's the plan Odysseus spoke of for getting into Troy; but how does it work? And what does the horse mean?'

'I don't know!' Helen wrung her hands as she gazed out of the window. 'My hopes have proved false so many times that I daren't, I can't believe it will succeed ... Look! There's the horse out in the middle of the plain: they're dragging it towards Troy.'

Nico looked, and saw a strange monster twenty feet or more in height, moving slowly and jerkily in the midst of a huge crowd of Trojans. As he and Helen watched, they could hear a confused babel of shouts and cheers, and sometimes snatches of song from those who laboured so strangely out there in the sweltering heat.

Slowly the horse drew nearer and nearer to Troy and was dragged on rollers up the slope to the Skaian Gate until it disappeared from their view round the corner of the tower. But as it went it was near enough for them to see the sun reflecting on the staring eyes of blood-red amethyst surrounded by sea-green beryl; the jagged teeth of splintered bone set in the open jaws, and the bronze-bound legs, and hooves of tortoise-shell. The wooden sides of the horse, curved like a ship, had been wreathed and draped with garlands and leaves by the rejoicing Trojans, and the ropes with which they were pulling it had been twined with threads of gold which glistened in the sun.

Late in the afternoon, when the shouts and songs told them that the horse was safely stabled in Troy, Deiphobus came again, wearing a wreath very much over one eye, and stumbling over his words from time to time.

'The horse is in the precinct of the Temple of Pallas Athena,' he told them. 'We had to pull down th'wall by the gate to get — to get it in. But it's safe now. An' Troy's safe now: the true horse and the true Palladion, side by side.' Deiphobus laughed drunkenly. 'The Greeks were deceived!' he said. 'Odysseus of the many wiles, indeed! They'll have to change his name to the much-duped Odysseus. Old Antenor and Theano, who've more courage than I thought they had, let him steal a copy of the Palladion and think it was the real thing. An' they had their quarrel over Palamedes, an' almost a civil war, and that clever Odysseus was suspected of being a cheat, when of course he was telling the ab'slute truth, because Palamedes *was* a traitor to them, an' was working for us, when he was paid enough. He helped us even when he was dead! It's because there was so much trouble, and such a quarrel among themselves that they gave up the siege and have gone home to Greece. Well done, Palamedes! I drink to his memory! Drink to him, you slut, or I'll thrash you tomorrow! Drink to him, Greek cub — you'll not get many more drinks!'

Evening closed in and night came on, to the wild revellings of the Trojans in the streets beyond the locked door of Helen's tower. Out on the plain odd bands came straggling home, and in the twilight several small companies of fighting men whom Priam or Deiphobus had sent out to scour the country round about so as to make sure that there was no sign of the Greeks anywhere.

Night fell, and the rejoicings of Troy faded to a tipsy murmur of sound, and died away into silence as the utter darkness closed in over the city and over the plain.

Helen filled her biggest lamp and set it in the middle of the wide windowsill, tending it carefully to make sure that as bright a flame as possible burnt constantly in it. The night was as still as death; not a breath stirred, and the flame burnt steadily without a flicker.

Time passed, while the sickening weight of suspense grew heavier and heavier, until Helen's nerve gave completely, and she sprang up and began pacing the room almost in frenzy.

'He won't come! He can't come!' she cried. 'Aphrodite, you have betrayed me again – you have always been my enemy. You gave me to Paris; you are giving me to Deiphobus, and it's Menelaus whom I love, only Menelaus. Nico, what shall I do? If he kills you, I'll throw myself out of that window . . . I might make a bargain with him – my life against yours. But he's a Trojan, and he'd break his word.'

Helen flung herself on the couch, and Nico strove to comfort her, though he was in sore need of comfort himself.

'I know Odysseus won't disappoint us, mother,' he repeated again and again. 'And he'll have told my father – Menelaus – about our danger; and *he* won't leave us either. He's out there somewhere, coming back to us.'

Nico leant out of the window beside the lamp. Far, far away there was a single red point of light, the only light in all that darkness.

'There's a watch fire out there,' he said, 'it's on the mound of earth near the coast where they buried the ashes of Achilles and Patroclus.'

'That'll be Sinon,' murmured Helen listlessly. 'Deiphobus said they wouldn't let him into Troy just yet: he said he smelt of drains.' She laughed drearily. 'But they gave him food and wine and built him a hut out there.'

158

'Someone's coming!' exclaimed Nico suddenly.

Helen listened for a moment, and then her face went white: 'Oh Zeus, it's Deiphobus,' she gasped. 'What shall I do? Zeus – Aphrodite, all you gods, have pity on us, and show me what to do.'

The stumbling steps drew nearer and nearer; they heard heavy breathing, and a fumbling with the bolts. Then the door creaked open and Deiphobus reeled into the room.

'All asleep!' he muttered, 'all Troy's asleep! But I'm not. I've come for my wife – and my revenge. Let's just tickle up the cub a little first. Time's up, and what does it matter whether we wait for Theano to mumble a few silly prayers and give us the marriage cup? I'll pour a marriage cup of our own – wine mingled with blood instead of water.'

He lurched across the room towards Nico. Helen caught him by the arm, but he struck at her, and as Nico sprang forward to protect her, seized him suddenly by the hair and tripped him up. Nico fell back across the couch, and Deiphobus fell with him, but without losing his grip, and Nico saw a knife shining in his right hand.

Wildly he struggled to hold it away from him as the point came nearer and nearer to his face. But he was no match for Deiphobus, who had been second in strength to Hector only among all the sons of Priam. Nearer and nearer came the cruel point, and Nico set his teeth to endure whatever was to happen: 'I mustn't cry out,' he told himself desperately. 'It'll spoil his sport, if nothing else . . . And I'm a Greek! I'm the son of Menelaus, King of Sparta!'

Suddenly, just as he felt that the knife must touch him, he heard Helen's voice, rich and sweet and thrilling:

'Deiphobus, my lord, my dear lord. Leave the boy; this is unworthy of you. You forget me, you forget that the sun will soon rise on your wedding-day, your wedding to Helen of Troy for whom the Greeks and the Trojans have fought a ten-year war — which *you* have won.'

'That's true,' said Deiphobus thickly. 'The cub can wait — it's Helen I want. She's my wife: Helen, who all the kings of Greece wanted to marry, and I've won her!' He let go of Nico, dropping his dagger as he did, and turned to Helen eagerly. She eluded him, but then took him gently by the hand.

'You know that I would have chosen to go back to Menelaus,' she said. 'I hoped that he would conquer Troy and take me home to Sparta. But he's deserted me, left me in Troy, and there's no help for it but to be your wife . . . And love is better than hate, isn't it?'

'Much better, Helen; I'm glad you're going to be sensible,' said Deiphobus, putting his arm round her.

'My lord,' said Helen, smiling sweetly up at him. 'Will you take me to see this strange and wonderful horse? All day you've been telling me about it, and I've been longing to see it . . . Take me now!'

Deiphobus stared about him stupidly for a minute or two; and then, leaning heavily on Helen, he turned towards the door.

'Why not?' he said thickly. 'Come on down into the precinct. The night's not as dark as it seems, and there's a flare by the Temple.'

They went out together and down the stairs, Helen talking quietly to Deiphobus all the time.

Nico sat up slowly and watched them go, his mind in a whirl. Helen was doing this to save him, of course . . .

But how could she act so convincingly? With a cold shiver he remembered how he had heard it said — perhaps Helen herself had said it — that when she followed Paris out from the palace of Menelaus at Sparta the spell of Aphrodite had fallen upon her so that she did not know what she was doing.

Nico went to the window. The lamp was burning brightly, and far away the red fire flickered on the Tomb of Achilles: but there was no sight or sound of any returning Greeks.

Then he stole to the door, which Deiphobus had closed after him. The wooden bolt was pushed across, but not tied with the leather thong. Nico picked up the knife which Deiphobus had dropped, and eased back the bolt without much difficulty. Then he went quietly out, down the stairs, and on to the wall above the Temple precinct.

Here he paused, and the unnatural intensity of the silence seemed to rise up and strike him in the face like a living thing. It seemed to hang over Troy, to press down on it like a stifling cloak: not even a dog barked.

Nico tiptoed down the steps, almost pushing through the silence as a swimmer pushes through water. By now he could see quite clearly, for the night was thick with stars, and, as Deiphobus had said, a great bowl of burning oil stood on a tripod in front of the Temple of Pallas.

When he reached the courtyard, he made his way round the edge to the back of the Temple, and then along under the shadow of the pillars on the farther side. As he came cautiously round the corner to the front of it he saw the horse standing out in the courtyard, grim and black in the light of the flare, and walking slowly round it were Helen and Deiphobus.

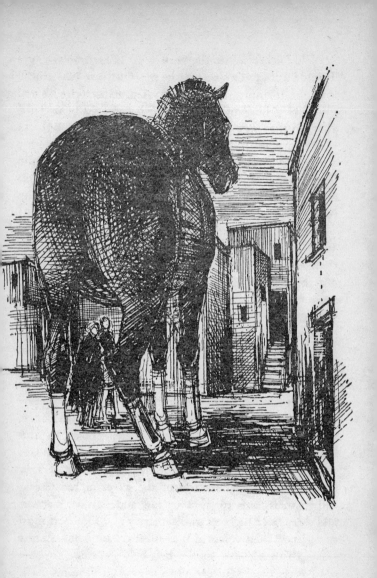

Nico backed under the portico by the entrance to the Temple so as to be sure that he was not seen. He glanced into the Temple, and then paused in surprise at the sound of a low voice whispering or praying behind the altar, in the inner shrine where the Palladion stood.

Overmastered by curiosity, and wondering whether after all Odysseus was leading the conquering Greeks into Troy by way of the drain, Nico tiptoed into the Temple and peeped round the edge of the altar on which the lamp burnt as usual.

The first thing he saw was that the two huge blocks of stone which had been placed over the drain after the theft of the Palladion were still in place. Then he made out the kneeling figures of two women: one he guessed must be Polyxena, for the other he knew by her voice to be Cassandra, Priam's priestess daughter.

'Apollo has deserted me,' Cassandra was saying. 'The gods have left Troy, and our doom is upon us. But thou, lady Athena, pure maiden Pallas, help me, preserve me from the hands of the enemy. I kneel before thine image, though it be no longer the very Palladion cast by thy hand from heaven. Lady Pallas, hear me. Hear me, maiden goddess, though there is no power in this Palladion which is no more than a lump of stone … Alas, alas, Troy is doomed indeed, for the Luck of Troy has left her … The voices of the wives of the Greeks call to their lords to lay Troy low and slay her warriors and carry her daughters into captivity … I knew it must be: I heard their voices as they must cry tonight — I knew them all in Helen's voice when first she came to Troy with Paris those ten long years ago … I gave my heart to a god who is the enemy of Troy; and you, Polyxena, little sister, gave yours to a man, the enemy of Troy.

Now they are both lost to us, and our doom is upon us: the double shame for me, and the cruel death by a woman's hand in far away Mycenae; honour and a quick death that shall never be forgotten for you. Achilles loved you, Polyxena — and you are nearer to him this night than even you were while he lived . . . But for me, for me — what do you hold in store, Apollo my lord and my destroyer?'

Cassandra's voice trailed away into inarticulate whispers, and Nico could hear Polyxena weeping quietly in the shadowy shrine.

'The Luck of Troy has indeed left her,' he found himself murmuring as he turned and stole with bowed head out of the Temple.

Outside as he stood under the portico and looked across the courtyard to the dark shape of the horse his thoughts were brought back to the happenings of the moment with a rush.

Helen and Deiphobus stood close together almost under the horse, and he was speaking to her in a low, thick voice from which Nico could not distinguish the words.

Suddenly Helen cried out into the oppressive silence:

'No, no, no! You shall not torture Nico! Never!' She clasped one leg of the horse, and looking up to it went on: 'Menelaus, my lord and my love! Hear me! Help me, save me, save our son from this devil! Come to me, Menelaus, for the sake of our love — for the sake of our son Nicostratus! Save him, even though you come to slay me as I deserve.'

Deiphobus laughed harshly. 'You may spare your prayers, Helen,' he exclaimed. 'Menelaus the coward is far away, running for Greece with his tail between his legs.

But tonight I rule Troy — and you — and his son and yours!'

Helen's voice changed suddenly: it became deeper and darker, with a touch of huskiness in it.

'Agamemnon!' she cried. 'King of men, ruler of Mycenae! Hear me! I call to you in the voice of Clytemnestra, your wife! For her sake hear me, and save us from this devil of Troy.'

'Agamemnon!' Deiphobus spat on the pavement. 'No use calling on him, he was the first to leave!'

Helen's voice grew gentle, shy, yet quietly insistent. 'My lord Odysseus,' she said. 'Come to us, Odysseus, for the sake of my cousin Penelope. Odysseus, your wife calls from distant Ithaca. Oh, have pity!'

Deiphobus muttered something under his breath, and caught hold of Helen roughly.

'Stop this nonsense and come with me!' he shouted. 'The boy may escape before we get there!' And tearing her away from the horse he began half dragging and half carrying her across the courtyard and up the steps towards the tower.

As they went Helen continued to cry out, now in one voice, now in another.

'Diomedes, help me! It is your wife Aegialeia who is suffering this! Help me, Anticlus, save Laodameia from shame! Help me, Idomeneus of Crete, help me for Meda's sake! Teucer, come to my aid —'

She was near the top of the steps by this time, and she ceased suddenly as Deiphobus struck her across the face, and they disappeared a moment later round the corner of the wall.

Nico would have rushed forward to his mother's aid, but something seemed to hold him back, to root him to the place where he stood. His eyes had followed Helen and Deiphobus until they were out of sight; now they turned back to the horse — and with a thrill of hope and fear he saw that something was happening, that Helen's prayers were being answered.

Underneath the rounded belly of the huge wooden shape the outline of a man appeared suddenly and fell with a thud to the pavement. A moment later a rope ladder dangled there and the short figure of Odysseus appeared scrambling down it.

With a low cry of joy Nico ran down the Temple steps and across the open courtyard. As he went he saw in the grey light of the coming day more and more men in armour that glimmered coldly in the thinning darkness appearing down the ladder from the horse.

One of these saw Nico, and with an exclamation whipped out his sword and sprang towards him. But Odysseus, who had been bending over Echion, the man who had jumped before the ladder was ready, saw and caught him by the arm as he would have lunged at Nico.

'No! Don't strike!' he exclaimed in his low, clear voice. 'Don't strike, Menelaus; it's your own son, Nicostratus!'

'Nicostratus! Nico!' The tall figure in the shining armour lowered his sword and stepped towards him with outstretched hand. Nico looked up into the kind, eager blue eyes that were so like his own, felt the strong hand fall and tremble on his shoulder, and stepped suddenly into a new world.

But the old world rushed back at him a moment later as he remembered.

'Father!' he exclaimed, the new word sounding strangely to his own ears, 'come quickly. Deiphobus. has dragged Helen – my mother – up to the tower. He's mad with drink, and he's the vilest devil in Troy even when he's sober. He's capable of anything, when he finds I'm not there for him to torture, as he planned to do.'

'All right.' Odysseus took quick command. 'Agamemnon, Menelaus and I are going straight to Helen's tower, you go to the Skaian Gate as we arranged and lead the men in. It's down over there, beyond where they broke the wall of the precinct to get the horse in. Come on, Nico, you can run fastest, as we both have armour: go on ahead – here, take this spare sword: I'm afraid Echion will have no further use for it. Hurry, we'll follow; I know the way!'

Up the steps went Nico, sword in hand, round the edge of the wall, and so to the entrance of the tower. At the door he paused a moment to look back, and as he did so the silence was broken suddenly by the crash of the Skaian Gate being flung open and the rush of feet up the steep street into the citadel, and past the citadel into the city of Troy.

As he dashed on up the stairs, past the little room where he could see Aethra sitting in her chair like a figure carved in stone, he could hear the first cries of alarm, the first shrieks of stricken Troy.

But he had no thought for the death-agony of Ilion as he pushed open the door and sprang into the room where Helen and Deiphobus struggled by the window – Helen to fling herself out, and Deiphobus to hold her back.

'Mother!' shouted Nico. 'We're saved! There's no need to die!'

'You cub!' hissed Deiphobus. 'I'll cut your heart out here and now!' As he spoke he flung Helen across the couch, whipped out his own sword, and rushed at Nico.

The bronze weapons clashed together; but Nico was no match for one of the best swordsmen in Troy. In one minute he was disarmed; in another he was lying on the floor while Deiphobus stood over him with sword drawn back to stab. But even in that moment the barbarian's lust for cruelty kept Deiphobus from delivering the final blow.

'Now, Nicostratus!' he cried exultantly. 'Look! I'll stab you just there, where it'll hurt most; and then there, where it means a slow but certain death; and there, so that you'll not be able to move from the floor. Are you ready? Look, my sword is drawn back for the first and cruellest blow –'

Deiphobus paused suddenly, his jaw dropped, his eyes filled slowly with fear and went wide as he looked across Nico to the doorway. Then he backed slowly towards the window where the lamp still burnt brightly, yellow against the coming grey of the dawn.

Nico twisted to one side and staggered to his feet, only to fall back on the end of the couch, realizing that he was wounded, though not seriously.

Now he saw that Menelaus stood in the doorway with his sword at the ready and the light of implacable hatred gleaming in his eyes.

'Deiphobus,' he said quietly, 'foul beast of Troy, your hour has come, caught like the evil rat that you are in my wife's room, about to torture my son.'

He moved slowly forward as he spoke. Deiphobus stooped suddenly, his hand behind him, and then swung round with a cry. A knife flashed across the room: Menelaus dodged, and it stood quivering in the door frame.

'Treacherous hound!' said Menelaus in a voice of

loathing. He struck, and the sword clattered to the ground from Deiphobus's hand. Then Deiphobus backed slowly away from him, his face ghastly with fear, back and back until he stood in front of the window, his shadow cast by the flickering lamp, towering huge and black over half the room.

For a moment there was complete stillness. Then Menelaus lunged, and sprang back with reddened sword. Deiphobus stood a moment more, then with a cry like that of a stricken wolf he fell backwards over the low sill across the lamp and disappeared with it on to the rocks far below.

Menelaus strode over to the window and looked down for a moment. Then he turned, the sword still in his hand, and took a step towards Helen as if he was half minded to kill her too.

But now she knelt before him in the clear, pale light of the awakening day, and the first flush of dawn flashed on the red Star Stone until once again the unstaining drops of blood seemed to fall from it, to fall and vanish and leave no mark.

The sword fell from Menelaus's hand and he held out his arms towards her.

'Helen!' he said.

In another moment she was in his arms, and the ten years were forgotten.

An hour later when Odysseus looked in, after showing Acamas and Demophon where to find their grandmother Aethra, he found Helen and Menelaus sitting hand in hand by the window while Nicostratus sat on the floor leaning against Helen's knee and looking up at Menelaus with happy eyes and his lips parted in eagerness as he listened to what his father was saying.

'Ah well,' said Odysseus, 'it's a good thing you have friends to fight your battles for you! No, stay where you are: it's all over. Troy is ours, the war's done, and we sail for Greece tomorrow.'

'Greece!' Nico breathed the name which had held so much of wonder and of longing for him since he could remember. And as Helen and Menelaus turned and looked out over the plain of Troy to where the blue Aegean gleamed and sparkled in the sunlight beyond the sand-dunes, he seemed to see with them golden Mycenae nestling on its hillside above the silver plain of Argos, Sparta in the wide green plain beneath the towering heights of snow-clad Taygetos, the deep blue bays, the tree-clad valleys and the soaring mountains of the loveliest land on earth.

AUTHOR'S NOTE

In this tale of the fall of Troy, the outline of the story is based on the myths and legends of Ancient Greece, while the background is supplied by the Homeric descriptions, the findings of archaeologists, and my own wanderings among the ruins of Mycenae, Troy and other Greek, Minoan and Mycenaean sites.

The legends followed in *The Luck of Troy* are taken from many and various Classical sources, beginning with Homer, and coming down to later poets and mythographers such as Quintus of Smyrna, Tryphiodorus, Apollodorus and even Dictys of Crete for the adventures of Palamedes, the love of Achilles and Polyxena, the theft of the Palladion, and the activities of Theano the priestess. It would be pointless to quote here from these authorities, or note where I have followed a less usual legend (as in the death of Deiphobus), where I have gone straight to Homer (as in the adventures of Odysseus when disguised as a beggar), and where I have put my own interpretation on traditions which conflict (as in the famous story of the 'letter' which caused Palamedes to be tried by the Greeks as a traitor).

One point, however, should be made clear. The actual part played in the story by Nicostratus is without direct authority from the ancient authors. It may, indeed, come as a surprise to many readers that Helen and Menelaus had a son: many authors mention only their daughter,

Hermione, who was left behind in Sparta. Nicostratus is, however, as genuine a character as any in the Tale of Troy. 'Now Menelaus had by Helen a daughter Hermione, and, according to some, a son Nicostratus,' says Apollodorus (*Library* III. xi. i). Homer only mentions Hermione; but Hesiod, who lived only a century or so later than the date usually ascribed to the final composition of the *Iliad*, declares: 'And Helen bare to Menelaus, famous with the spear, Hermione, and her youngest born, Nicostratus – that valiant warrior.' We know from another early writer, Stasinus, that Helen took her son with her when Paris carried her off to Troy. Several other authors mention Nicostratus, but unfortunately no legends survive of what he did at Troy, or of what became of him after the end of the siege – though he apparently came home safely to Sparta, and was venerated there as a hero.

I have endeavoured to fill in this gap, trying to present the last year of the Siege of Troy as it would have appeared to this Greek boy of twelve or thirteen who had such exceptional opportunities of observing all that happened. There were 'eye-witness' accounts written in Greek more than two thousand years ago, which are now lost; but Latin versions of them, said to have been made while Nero was emperor of Rome, still survive – their 'authors' being Dictys, a follower of Idomeneus the King of Crete, and Dares the Phrygian who fought on the Trojan side. In this way, too, *The Luck of Troy* has full Classical authority!

R.L.G.

Heard about the Puffin Club?

... it's a way of finding out more about Puffin
books and authors, of winning prizes (in
competitions), sharing jokes, a secret code, and
perhaps seeing your name in print! When you
join you get a copy of our magazine, *Puffin
Post*, sent to you four times a year, a badge
and a membership book.
For details of subscription and an application
form, send a stamped addressed envelope to:

The Puffin Club Dept A
Penguin Books Limited
Bath Road
Harmondsworth
Middlesex UB7 0DA

and if you live in Australia, please write to:

The Australian Puffin Club
Penguin Books Australia Limited
P.O. Box 257
Ringwood
Victoria 3134